New Library of Pa
GENERAL EDITOR: DEREK BLOWS

Derek Blows is the Director of the Westminster Pastoral
Foundation and a psychotherapist at University College
Hospital. He is also an honorary canon of Southwark
Cathedral.

Holding in Trust

Titles in this series include:

Still Small Voice: An Introduction to Counselling
MICHAEL JACOBS

Letting Go: Caring for the Dying and Bereaved
PETER SPECK AND IAN AINSWORTH-SMITH

Living Alone: The Inward Journey to Fellowship
MARTIN ISRAEL

Invisible Barriers: Pastoral Care with Physically Disabled People
JESSIE VAN DONGEN-GARRAD

Learning to Care: Christian Reflection on Pastoral Practice
MICHAEL H. TAYLOR

Liberating God: Private Care and Public Struggle
PETER SELBY

Make or Break: An Introduction to Marriage Counselling
JACK DOMINIAN

Meaning in Madness: The Pastor and the Mentally Ill
JOHN FOSKETT

Paid to Care?: The Limits of Professionalism in Pastoral Care
ALASTAIR V. CAMPBELL

Swift to Hear: Facilitating Skills in Listening and Responding
MICHAEL JACOBS

Brief Encounters: Pastoral Ministry through the Occasional Offices
WESLEY CARR

Love the Stranger: Ministry in Multi-Faith Areas
ROGER HOOKER AND CHRISTOPHER LAMB

Being There: Pastoral Care in Time of Illness
PETER SPECK

Going Somewhere: People with Mental Handicaps and their Pastoral Care
SHEILA HOLLINS AND MARGARET GRIMER

Made in Heaven?: Ministry with Those Intending Marriage
PETER CHAMBERS

Family Matters: The Pastoral Care of Personal Relationships
SUE WALROND-SKINNER

Helping the Helpers: Supervision and Pastoral Care
JOHN FOSKETT AND DAVID LYALL

*The Pastor as Theologian: The Integration of Pastoral Ministry,
Theology and Discipleship*
WESLEY CARR

City of God?: Pastoral Care in the Inner City
NICHOLAS BRADBURY

Clergy Stress: The Hidden Conflicts in Ministry
MARY ANNE COATE

A Dictionary of Pastoral Care
edited by ALASTAIR V. CAMPBELL

New Library of Pastoral Care
GENERAL EDITOR: DEREK BLOWS

———

HOLDING IN TRUST

The Appraisal of Ministry

———

Michael Jacobs

First published in Great Britain 1989
SPCK
Holy Trinity Church
Marylebone Road
London NW1 4DU

British Library Cataloguing in Publication Data

Jacobs, Michael *1941—*
    Holding in trust: the appraisal of ministry.
    1. Christian church. Ministry
    I. Title   II. Series
    262'.14

    ISBN 0-281-04438-4

            Filmset by Pioneer, Perthshire
            Printed in Great Britain by
            the Courier Press, Tiptree

Contents

Foreword *by Derek Blows*   vii

Preface   ix

1 Accountability and Acceptance   1

2 Precedents and Parallels   18

3 Principles and Practices   51

4 Radical Reviews   78

5 Acknowledging Anxieties   93

6 Insights into Interviewing   114

7 Specific Suggestions   133

8 Attraction and Alienation   149

9 Larger Lenses   165

Bibliography   179

Index   182

Foreword

The *New Library of Pastoral Care* has been planned to meet the needs of those people concerned with pastoral care, whether clergy or lay, who seek to improve their knowledge and skills in this field. Equally, it is hoped that it may prove useful to those secular helpers who may wish to understand the role of the pastor.

Pastoral care in every age has drawn from contemporary secular knowledge to inform its understanding of men and women and their various needs and of the ways in which these needs might be met. Today it is perhaps the secular helping professions of social work, counselling and psycho-therapy, and community development which have particular contributions to make to pastors in their work. Such knowledge does not stand still, and pastors would have a struggle to keep up with the endless tide of new developments which pour out from these and other disciplines, and to sort out which ideas and practices might be relevant to their particular pastoral needs. Among present-day ideas, for instance, of particular value might be an understanding of the social context of the pastoral task, the dynamics of the helping relationship, the attitudes and skills as well as factual knowledge which might make for effective pastoral inter-vention and, perhaps most significant of all, the study of particular cases, whether through verbatim reports of inter-views or general case presentation. The discovery of ways of learning from what one is doing is becoming increasingly important.

There is always a danger that a pastor who drinks deeply at the well of a secular discipline may risk losing a distinct pastoral identity and become 'just another' social worker or counsellor. It in no way detracts from the value of these professions to assert that the role and task of the pastor are quite unique among the helping professions and deserve to be clarified and strengthened rather than weakened. The theological commitment of the pastors and the appropriate use of their role will be a recurrent theme of the series. At the same time pastors cannot afford to work in a vacuum. They need to be able to communicate and co-operate with those helpers in other disciplines whose work may overlap, without loss of their own unique status. This in turn will mean being able to communicate with them through some understanding of their concepts and language.

Finally, there is a rich variety of styles and approaches in pastoral work within the various religious traditions. No attempt will be made to secure a uniform approach. The Library will contain the variety, and even perhaps occasional eccentricity, which such a title suggests. Some books will be more specifically theological and others more concerned with particular areas of need or practice. It is hoped that all of them will have a usefulness that will reach right across the boundaries of religious denomination.

DEREK BLOWS
Series Editor

Preface

Appraisal in the context of the Church may be as new to the reader as it was to me when I started researching this book. Perhaps some will feel, as I acknowledge in these pages, that to engage in formal work evaluation is to model the Church (in their eyes inappropriately) upon the ways of mammon. Others will perhaps welcome some attempt to order the complexities of ministry in the modern world and come to realize, as I myself did, that the value of appraisal extends much further than commerce and industry, and beyond increased productivity, the free market and the profit motive.

Some of my readers will have heard of little other than Joint Work Consultation, one of the first appraisal schemes, promoted by the Anglican Diocese of Liverpool. Or they may have heard of schemes nearer home and may even have begun to take part in them. The scene is changing rapidly. When I started researching this book I thought there was virtually no appraisal in the Church, and clearly some of my correspondents felt the same. But one piece of information led on to another, one person recommended that I get in touch with someone else, and in a matter of weeks I had built up a large file of material—private papers, proposals for schemes that may or may not have got off the ground, confidential reports, and forms of appraisal—from a variety of sources. There will be few now who are not aware that appraisal is round the corner. I hope that this book will help clarify some of the issues, so that those who promote, design, service and take part in appraisal procedures can usefully engage in the development of the most appropriate methods for the Church.

I have come to see appraisal in this context as being about more than the appraisal of clergy. I have myself been asked to help design a form of appraisal for readers in one diocese.

Some local churches or church centres employ and supervise lay ministers and other personnel, and so may wish to design appraisal procedures for them and with them. Review of other wider aspects of church life is also important, as I suggest in the last chapter. I hope the principles and questions which arise from this study of appraisal will be of value in furthering the self-examination of work and ministry at all levels of church life.

I have been overwhelmed by the generosity of responses from those to whom I have written in search of material on appraisal procedures. This is an opportunity to thank the following, but also anyone whom I may have inadvertently omitted, or who has taken part more generally in consultations at which I have been present, and from which I may have gleaned ideas: Canon John Atherton, Revd Derek Atkinson, Revd David Barker and staff at ACCM, Revd Chris Beales, Canon Bernard Brown, Fr Gerard Burke, Canon Tony Chesterman, Diocese of Derby Readers Board, Revd Alan Duce, Canon Eric Forshaw, Canon Ian Hardaker, Rt Revd Robert Hardy, Revd Tim Herbert, Dr Sarah Horsman and the Society of Mary and Martha, Mr Bernard Kilroy, Archdeacon Christopher Laurence, Mr Antony Lawton, Canon Christopher Lewis, Alison McKay, Revd Fraser Maclennan, Revd Terry Oakley, Revd Clive Raybould, Revd Robert Reiss, Revd Paul Skirrow, Archdeacon Leslie Stanbridge, Canon Vincent Strudwick, Revd David Swain, Canon Dr Norman Todd and Revd John Tomlinson.

Simply to say thank you is in fact a weak repayment of a debt to these colleagues, friends or relative strangers, who have lent me sections of their theses or dissertations, photocopied papers, read and commented on my draft chapters, provided me with time for interviews or given up time to write at length, and given their own analyses of the problems and opportunities that arise from appraisal. Such free pooling of experience and knowledge is a humbling experience for a writer, who in the end is one who receives any credit. While I cannot blame any of them for any mistakes of fact or judgement that appear in these pages, I would wish anything that is helpful to be attributed to them as well. Their co-operation is an example of the best aspects of the appraisal of ministry: the mutual sharing of our expertise to the furtherance of the ministry of others and, in the end, to the extension of the Kingdom of God.

Michael Jacobs
Tugby, Leicestershire
March 1989

ONE

Accountability and Acceptance

Writing about assessment, or as I shall more often call it, appraisal, is like writing a book on the advantages of regular dental check-ups: such things may be necessary (evils?) but let us not dwell on them more than we need. Some aspects of life are best got over and done with; least mentioned, soonest forgotten.

Many aspects of pastoral care and counselling represented by the New Library of Pastoral Care series carry both the interest and value of enabling the clerical or lay minister to care for others; such, after all, is one of her or his major aims in ministry. Caring for others, as I have observed elsewhere,[1] whatever merits it has in itself, also has the effect of shifting attention away from our own needs or, on occasion, from our own difficulties. But appraisal or assessment focuses on the minister, and carries with it the risk of discovering something unwelcome about him- or herself. So, browsing reader, if you feel threatened, close the covers now, and put the book back on the shelf! It is beginning to feel as if the cover should carry a health warning!

Sadly and commonly, such is our picture of assessment — it will be painful and critical, and will expose us to shame, guilt or fear. Our images of assessment are often heavily influenced by biblical scenes of judgement, or by medieval theologies of hell-fire and agonizing torture of the soul — compared to which the dentist's chair is a luxurious massage. What is worse, appraisal is fast becoming if not a compulsory exercise in ministry, then at least one with strong moral pressure to submit to it. Better perhaps to go through it without thinking too much about it and then get on with the real job?

1

Theology and appraisal

Such pictures of judgement are scarcely surprising, given both a long tradition which has emphasized the assessment at the Last Day, and also some of the more lurid scenes which eschatological parables, visions or preaching have promoted. But I overdo the imagery deliberately, because there is so much more to the biblical picture of judgement than that of reward or punishment, heavenly choirs or the gnashing of teeth. Both Old and New Testaments stress the idea of stewardship, of men and women caring for God's creation, exercising a ministry on God's behalf and using to the full their natural gifts and acquired skills. Adam is given dominion over creation and his responsibility to name the living creatures demonstrates how God hands power over to mankind. In so many of the Gospel parables servants are entrusted with financial, domestic or agricultural tasks; and perhaps the emphasis is more on their readiness to take on such responsibilities (even at the risk of failing) than on the return for their labours. The wise are those who are ready and alert and have not hidden themselves when the Lord comes; the timid and the reluctant and the careless are pictured as foolish.

To be sure, there are places where God's judgement is terrifying in its sadistic cruelty and torture. But even where this is seen at its most extreme, such as the vision of wrath in Isaiah 34, it is the same God who is described in the following chapter as bringing recompense also, so that the eyes of the blind shall be opened, the ears of the deaf unstopped: the lame man shall leap as the hart, the tongue of the dumb shall sing and waters shall break out in the wilderness. Judgement can be affirming, healing and creative and need not always be destructive. Very often it is not the poor, the weak, the humble, the apparently low achievers in society who have anything to fear; instead it is those who are not just strong but who boast of their strength and who depend on themselves alone, who tend to reap the most scorn when it comes to judgement. Furthermore a true theology of grace does not make salvation and sanctification depend upon success or failure, at least as the world understands those terms.

I deliberately raise these questions because fear of judgement is perhaps the greatest barrier to effective appraisal. I return to look at this in more detail in Chapter 6, when I look at fear of God's judgement being extended to anxieties about being judged by those who conduct appraisals. When we think about appraisal it is these negative fears of what it is about and what it will do to our self-esteem that come to the fore. No wonder there is such suspicion and defensiveness when appraisal is suggested, whether those who are asked to take part in it are clergy, teachers, or any other professionals. It is not simply that the subject smacks of business and industry. Unfortunately such negative views obscure the real value and the positive features which come from taking part in regular ministerial review.

Theologically the notion of accountability and consequent judgement of one's stewardship provides one of the supports for the introduction of appraisal. The all-or-nothing quality of the Last Judgement has been largely replaced in our own times by a sense of being under continuous judgement, so that it is more fitting that appraisal of ministry should take place periodically, while we can still take notice of it, rather than in an obituary column.

It is, of course, not possible to write a theology of appraisal, but theology can inform appraisal, just as theology informs pastoral care and counselling. A further theological aspect which helps us to look at appraisal is that of individual ministry as being an integral part of the whole Body of Christ. Writing of theology and collaborative ministry, Michael Taylor reminds us that the great biblical and doctrinal themes, from creation to eschatology, speak of working together; that members of the Church are described as being as members of one body; and that central to affirmations about human beings and indeed the Godhead are notions of love and relationships.[2]

Taylor particularly concentrates upon the need for co-operativeness in appraisal because we need one another to help us see more clearly—just as in counselling there is a crucial role for the counsellor as an outside observer. In counselling it is stressed that left to ourselves we have an infinite capacity for self-deception which an outsider may help us to question. Taylor makes the same point, from a theological point of view, when he writes that the outside observer is necessary because a realistic assessment of ourselves is made difficult through sin. Sin blinds us to ourselves as we really are, sometimes because we overestimate our goodness and at other times because we are unable to see ourselves as adequate. Creatureliness implies limitations, so 'we do not see the whole'.[3]

Taylor reminds us that sin means we are bound to fail at times and that there will inevitably be flaws in our work. Having someone to help us review our work does not mean that we put that person in a position of judgement over us, because the Christian gospel asserts the absence of 'pecking orders' and 'class distinctions' and comes out strongly against anyone doing the judging other than God. However, if we see appraisal as part of collaborative ministry, the person who assists appraisal does not have to be viewed as 'over-against-us' but as someone who aids our own self-examination. These observations are particularly pertinent to the debate, which I later examine, as to whether appraisal is part of line-management (in which case judgements may well be made by those above us in the pecking order) or whether, inasmuch as being part of the Body can ever permit such a view, it is for the individual minister alone.

Taylor also argues that an understanding of sin means that we cannot be left to our own devices: 'The doctrine of sin . . . may be used to argue in favour of not being left to ourselves without the checks and balances that others provide.'[4] Likewise the Church, even though in one respect it belongs to the City of God, also has its fair share of the problems of the earthly city, and so, Taylor writes, we may need 'to accept the need for structures which provide some protections against irresponsibility and the neglect and misuse of our freedom.'[5]

Taylor's short but valuable essay includes a further theological observation which deserves repeating. The author says that putting the gospel first means that we may have to put ourselves at risk, and that this includes putting ourselves at the risk of another's gaze, in order to be more effective in our working out of the gospel in ministry. Eschatology too, he says, tells us that we live in a time before the end and we should not get too frustrated at being unable to achieve all that we would wish. So while appraisal helps us to affirm our strengths, a true eschatology also affirms our inability to achieve everything we would want. 'The best we can envisage . . . must for ever disturb the best we can achieve and provoke us out of self-satisfaction into achieving something better.'[6] The doctrine of the end acts as a spur to an even deeper vision of what we would like to help bring about: in ourselves, in the Church, and in the world. I include this telling point with some trepidation, because I do not wish to overwhelm the reader with such a vision before having come through that crucial first stage which sets to rest the fear of being criticized and judged. Visions and ideals are very important and fine, but only when we have moved beyond that point where we flagellate ourselves for failing to achieve or reach them!

There are further aspects of the theology of ministry, and of ministry as being part of the one Body, that reflect upon the value and justification of appraisal. Membership of the Body means that my own life and ministry inevitably affects others who belong to the same Body. The psychological parallel to this is systems theory, which helps to explain how families, groups and organizations function as part of a continuously self-balancing system, in which action and therefore movement on or by one part inevitably sets the other parts in motion, to restore the balance of the system.[7] Part of my responsibility for others therefore extends to responsibility for my own life and ministry as always in some way impinging on them. Review of ministry is thus of potential value to more than the individual; done well it will affect not only those with whom I work directly but also the Church as a whole.

Within episcopal Churches ministry is essentially seen, theologically, as being a co-operative ministry between bishop and presbyters. In the new Anglican ordination service there is the same sense of holding in trust that I have referred to above in relation to the biblical ideas of stewardship: 'The treasure now to be entrusted to you is Christ's flock.'[8] But the joint ministry is made even clearer in the expression which a bishop uses of the work of a new incumbent in a parish: 'Your cure and mine'. Such a notion of shared ministry provides real justification for the bishop's involvement in appraisal, even though, as later chapters will spell out, there may also be difficulties in an appraisal scheme which is episcopally led. From the non-episcopal Churches we have a different but equally valuable insight, that of the shared ministry of minister and people, and the greater emphasis on the priesthood of all believers. This further, theologically-based, sense of order reminds us that appraisal should also in some respect involve the congregations in which ministers serve. Their part in appraisal is not simply that of assessing the work of their minister, but of discovering where he or she needs their support in sharing in active ministry.

Shared ministry in the Church is an expression of the sharing in God's responsibility for creation that has been referred to above. The relevance of theology to appraisal might be concluded with an iconographic representation of the Creation story. God is anthropomorphically depicted as lying in bed with what looks like the world in his hand, resting on the seventh day and seeing that 'it was good'.[9] Such a positively charming image of the Creator perhaps provides that warmth, restfulness and affirmation with which to approach what seems otherwise to be a potentially threatening area of ministry.

The advantages and applications of appraisal

To take time to review one's work, like God resting on the seventh day, is valuable in itself. It enables personal strengths and achievements to be recognized and apparently less successful areas of ministry to be accepted. An appraiser can provide affirmation and support, as well as permission not to have to be perfect in all things; he or she can challenge some of the fantasies about the job; this should encourage the person appraised to be more realistic and objective, and possibly therefore to cease making unrealistic and unrealizable demands upon himself. The presence of an assistant—an 'appraiser' or a 'consultant' — need not be felt as a threat, but as an encouragement and as building confidence. He or she can often identify more precisely what is and what is not possible in a given situation and what opportunities and limitations are present in the minister, the place, or the people.

Appraisal can, however, have a ripple effect. Hopefully the consequences of appraisal will reach the minister's family, for example in the review of opportunities for recreational and family life, as well as of time spent at work. The fact that their minister assesses her or his ministry may help church councils and congregations to evaluate the local church's ministry as a whole; and laity who know that appraisal is taking place might be more open to change and to parish or local church audit, as examined in Chapter 9. Part of the change that may arise is the delegation or sharing of ministry. Realistic expectations can encourage others to participate more fully in church life. More widely still, there can also be a potentially valuable feedback to a diocese, province or district about the general perceptions, problems and experience of ministry in a particular area, or under a particular management structure. This means safeguarding the confidentiality of individual appraisal by collating information anonymously, perhaps through a body of 'consultants'. Appraisal may, then, lead to more targetted in-service training for ministry, but may also result in other areas of general concern being at the least raised and at best rectified.

Standing back from day-to-day ministry provides an opportunity for greater awareness of the shape of a person's work, and a chance to take a medium- to long-term view. Talking in detail about one's ministry may even help some people to overcome their self-imposed sense of isolation. Skilfully handled, appraisal can also help ministers to greater honesty about themselves, their church and their ministry and to deeper self-knowledge and self-discovery.

It should be obvious that while the term itself may be new, there is nothing startlingly original about appraisal. It is a particular method of reviewing ministry and of reviewing the self in ministry based upon already existent self-awareness. Such self-awareness has always been part of another formal

practice—spiritual direction. Although the latter may historic-
ally have concentrated more upon the minister's prayer life,
inevitably spiritual life is affected by, and in turn affects, the
whole of ministry. Spiritual direction at its best is also
concerned with the whole person and the whole ministry.

In most people there already exists a type of inner dialogue
which takes place at intervals during every waking day (and
indeed, at another level, in dreamlife too). We reflect upon
ourselves and upon those we meet during the course of a day,
assessing ourselves and them, observing the effect of
conversation on each other, and adapting what we say and
how we behave to the observations that come from our
internal monitoring. For the most part this is an unobtrusive,
relaxed and natural reflection upon what is happening to us
and within us as we move in and out of pastoral, social and
family encounters. Only if something seems particularly
difficult to handle do we become aware of a more pressing
need to try and assess or appraise what is happening.

In the course of a day's ministry, for example, we have
probably reflected on the different activities and interactions
in which we have been involved. These reflections are likely
to include such personal assessments as 'That visit to Mrs X
seemed to go well . . . I think I helped Mr Y . . . Z helped me to
understand more about what it is like to be housebound.'
Those who are able to look at their mistakes as well as their
successes may also reflect more critically on some situations:
'I'm not very happy about the way I handled that . . . I wish
now that I had said such-and-such . . . I must remember next
time to do this or that.' This type of self-assessment in daily
ministry provides us with opportunities for some necessary
self-satisfaction, and either reassures us (where things have
gone well) or helps us to plan ahead for a different approach
(when we are less than happy with the present results).

I stress this review of ministry as a process which goes on
all the time in order to demonstrate how the theme of this
book simply builds upon an internal process. Of course this
internal process is by and large safer when it is part of a
more public exercise, whether by 'public' we mean speaking
(albeit confidentially) in the presence of a single consultant,

or the type of appraisal which leads to a report going on file in the bishop's office.

The formalization of the internal process creates some problems which need to be overcome if appraisal is to serve the interests of the individual and the institution equally well. Perhaps, therefore, the more appropriate analogy for appraisal is not the informal and continuous assessment of the day's events (where the less palatable side can be more easily forgotten!), so much as the formal type of self-examination which is included in most traditional Catholic manuals for private prayer. Many of my readers will not be used to such a tradition, but there is a parallel between appraisal and the regular self-examination which is suggested as part of the structure of daily prayer, as well as self-examination before the sacrament of penance or reconciliation. One less than helpful parallel is the anxiety that might accompany both exercises, and the feelings of guilt that might be engendered by self-examination. Appraisal needs to be as honest as self-examination, but I think neither activity is beneficial if it leads to over-anxiousness or to a burden of guilt or shame. Another less than helpful aspect of this parallel might also be that of working through a list of 'sins' in the case of the sacrament of penance, and a list of pre-set questions in appraisal, in an obsessional manner. Although I later suggest a list of questions appropriate for self-appraisal, I would not wish the list to become an examination paper where every question must be answered!

This, of course, is a parallel from the privacy of our own thoughts and our own spiritual discipline. But a more public and more formal parallel already takes place in every church (whether or not a scheme for appraisal of work and ministry has yet been introduced) in the writing of reports for the annual church meeting; in Anglican churches there is also the quinquennial inspection, another way of conducting a type of appraisal, which these days is not limited as it once was to finance and church plant. Accountability is formalized in every organization which has a constitution, and when used constructively serves as an occasion for review as well as report.

Each of these parallels—private reflection and the public annual report—has its limitations as an analogy for appraisal. What they do demonstrate is that appraisal has many different dimensions; following on from the image of the 'ripple effect' of appraisal which I have used above, it is important to raise a question—which is not easily answered—as to the boundaries of self-reflection, self-appraisal, more formal appraisal, and the wider reviews of policy which take place in churches at local, area and national level. In the next chapter I shall attempt to formulate some definitions of the different terms which can be used, but here it is valuable to illustrate the essential interconnection of these different aspects (Figure 1). They are pictured as a series of concentric circles, starting in the middle with the personal inner self and expanding outwards to include reviews of the life of the whole Church, carried out through reports and working parties, synodical debates, conferences, commissions and the like. Such a diagram places the self at the centre, and will provoke some objections from those who feel that God should be placed at the centre. This raises all manner of theological and psychological questions which I do not propose to discuss here, except to observe that if the reader wishes to place God in the diagram, whether at the centre or as encompassing the whole, or both, that is fine; but we might also raise the question, which again I shall not attempt to answer, as to who appraises God?

The innermost circles represent the personal life of the minister, and are divided into the inner self and the more conscious self. Each of these circles represents aspects which are so personal and intimate that they are not normally appropriate areas for the type of appraisal which I have in mind in this book. Indeed I imagine that very few people choose to look closely at the innermost circle, the largely unconscious inner self, unless a major crisis forces them to do so. Nevertheless, reflection upon this inner self will be familiar to those who have experience of some sort of self-examination or self-analysis, spiritual direction, personal counselling and psychotherapy. These types of self-reflection (with or without the help of another person) all in their various ways serve the purpose of nourishing the growth of

Figure 1: The concentric circles of appraisal

the inner self from which, of course, all else springs, even though in turn that inner self needs the 'facilitating environment' of the outer circles for such growth to take place. We need to remember that unlike ripples on a pond, these particular concentric circles influence and move each other.

I repeat that this particular area is not the concern of this book, nor should it be the main subject of self-appraisal as defined here. It is however possible that the process of appraisal or assessment will reveal the value (or even the need) of developing this type of self-reflection, so that a person can look more closely at her or his personal and spiritual life in another setting and with a different kind of helper, one who is particularly skilled in spiritual direction, counselling or psychotherapy.

However, strong though my reservation is about appraisal becoming a psychotherapeutic relationship, I cannot pretend that the minister is not an ordinary person, subject to all the joys and distresses, pains and pleasures, stresses and opportunities that being human entails. Inevitably in appraisal questions will be raised from time to time which may need to be examined more closely in another setting; examples of these questions are found in a theological college's guide to self-assessment.[10] The opening section is called 'The minister as person' and proposes questions relating to the balance between being and doing, and personal qualities such as love, authority, humility, etc. The ultimate question 'Who am I?' which might be addressed to the inner circle, may not so easily be excluded from the overall aim of self-appraisal, although it is likely to be the more conscious self in the second circle from the centre which will from time to time need to be linked to the other outer circles. Furthermore, since these concentric circles interrelate, the way a person sees him- or herself will influence the way in which appraisal of some of the 'outer' areas will be approached. The person who answers the question 'Who am I?' either in defensively confident tones or with the note of low self-esteem, may well approach appraisal with dread, and react to any comment negatively, as being confirmation of his or her own self-criticism. The person whose inner self is receptive to and not perturbed by different dimensions of experience, who can for instance accept another person's comment as having a certain kind of validity and authority, may well benefit greatly from the experience. I shall look at some aspects of this in Chapter 6, where I shall examine some of the personal difficulties that might stand in the way of open and useful appraisal.

The third circle outwards is one which includes the minister in relation to her or his family, to close friends, and in social settings. I include this circle since it is obviously, for many people, the 'base' upon which they are able to build other work relationships, as well as more obviously the 'base' from which they set out to work and to which they return after work. In the case of the clergy there is, however, the additional factor that this base is nearly always also their workplace, and therefore it is highly probable that partner and family (whether they like it or not) will be caught up in the minister's working life. So while these relationships are not strictly part of a self-appraisal scheme, not only does reflection on everyday life inevitably have to take account of them, but any more formal systems of appraisal must somewhere make room for the influence of this third circle and the next (day-to-day work) upon each other. The relationships within this third circle (if they mean anything at all) probably provide the most honest, sometimes painfully honest, expressions of a person's work, and may therefore have their own part to play in appraisal. Nevertheless in any other profession it is doubtful whether a person's family and social life would have much place in appraisal and assessment. In spiritual direction or pastoral counselling such areas may have their place, but in work appraisal they need to be handled with even greater care if they are not to be felt to be intrusive.

There are some issues which are appropriate for appraisal and others which are not, unless they are raised by the person being appraised as a request for further help. The use of time, decisions about moves (especially with regard to education or the partner's own work and career plans) and some other family concerns are relevant to appraisal. Areas which concern the actual relationships within the family are not. It is therefore not surprising that in another section of the theological college guide to self-assessment already referred to, where questions are asked about relationships, they address the professional level; but they do include management of time, recreation, and family finances as part of that system of self-appraisal. If some of these questions seem potentially uncomfortable for those who are being appraised, we also need to consider that some of the answers (particularly about standards of accommodation, lack of office space, the blurred boundaries between family and work where both are based in the same house) might also raise serious questions for the employing churches and could involve considerable financial problems if they were to be properly addressed! Appraisal of this area of life may enable clergy to raise rather more forcibly some of the constraints upon them which come from 'living on the job'.

The fourth circle begins to move more obviously into the

working part of a person's life and their day-to-day ministry. It is here that the sort of overview which this book addresses really begins to come into its own. I do not therefore want to anticipate the questions that might be asked in this area, although it is valuable to make a clear distinction between the different types of question that can be asked in appraisal; some are appropriate to detailed work consultancy, some are appropriate to personal development, and others are relevant both to these and also to the more formal 'line management' type of appraisal. Some questions are concerned with here and now issues, others are aimed at looking at the type of future developments that the fifth circle includes. Thus 'How do you spend your time during the week? Are there adjustments you might make to the balance of pastoral work, administration, and private study?' are questions aimed at the immediate situation. 'What would you like to be doing in five years' time? How might you prepare for that?' are more long-term questions. 'What are your strong points? What gifts do you have for different forms of ministry? How might any particular area be developed for the future?' form yet a third set of questions showing the overlap between the two circles.

Thus the fifth circle remains with individual ministry but takes a further step back from it, to look at where a person's ministerial development is taking them. Here the questions are more concerned with mid- to long-term issues, and are probably more forward-looking, whereas questions in appraisal addressing the fourth circle concerns are likely to demand analysis of the immediate past and the present. Mid-term issues include questions such as: 'Can you suggest any specific targets (for you, for the parish) to be achieved by next year?' Longer-term questions involve those already mentioned above such as: 'How do you want to see your ministry develop?' In the answers to such questions the appraiser might need to help identify training and developmental needs, but the employing institution will probably have to respond by providing the means to enable such development (where appropriate to both minister and church) to take place.

Particularly as we move into this fifth circle, we find that there are issues arising which are not confined to the minister, and which indeed are not always in the power or ability of the minister to see through. Others are involved: those who train, support and deploy ministers, whether they be bishops, moderators or superintendents, or those boards and committees which have special responsibility for lay ministers such as readers or local preachers. If we wish people to develop their ministry and seek to involve them in their development, we will need others who can provide the resources and who can encourage them to develop in ways which serve their own needs as well as those of the Church as a whole. At this point appraisal, especially if it has been a private one, may need to be shared, at least in some of its aspects, with a diocesan or provincial official, or even with the senior staff of a diocese or an area. When it comes to long-term development, an individual may identify the doors that could be opened but it is often others who hold the keys to such possibilities.

I have already briefly alluded to two of the most vexatious questions about appraisal in the Church: whether or not it should be carried out by those in authority in a diocese or area, and whether it should be compulsory or not. Without developing those questions at this point of the book, it is clear that as appraisal addresses this fifth circle of mid-term and long-term ministerial development it is dealing with information which is of relevance to the employing institution as well as to the individual minister. Whether or not appraisal takes place, the senior officers of an institution like the Church are making assessments (at the least privately in their minds) of the ministers for whom they are responsible, either through direct knowledge or by repute. Appraisal, particularly when some aspects of it can be shared with a higher authority, ensures that such information is more out in the open, that 'myths' can be checked out, and that misinformation can be corrected.

The three outer circles put the minister more obviously in the context of the parish, the deanery or district, the diocese or the province, and the Church as a whole. Self-appraisal, if it is effectively carried out, will hopefully help to bring about change not only in the person concerned but also in the context in which he or she works. While we sometimes need to change ourselves, there are also times when we need to alter our circumstances, particularly if we are to maximize internal change. It is, for instance, one thing to realize that I need to do less, or more, or do things differently in my ministry, but another thing to change the expectations of those around me; and I may well need their assistance or that of my fellow ministers to help work out a more effective role. Or it is one thing to recognize that I want to encourage more indigenous leadership in my local church, but quite another to have lay training resources to assist me. Appraisal may therefore mean identifying resources, and where they appear not to exist it may lead to encouragement to make them available. Again we see how appraisal can lead to our addressing questions to others, especially to those who assume some responsibility for our ministry. If appraisal is carried out extensively in a diocese or some other ecclesiastical area, it may also yield the same type of questions and similar observations from widely different viewpoints, and so compel an institution to look at the need to change its own structures. This will be especially relevant if there is any anonymous pooling of ideas by those responsible for conducting or assisting appraisal and assessment. I refer to this above in considering the 'ripple' effect of appraisal. Since I have already argued that appraisal is part of the shared ministry of (in episcopal terms) bishop, priest and people, then appraisal of the individual minister, if it is to be at all effective, must influence (again in episcopal terms) both the diocese and the parish.

I include these circles, however, not simply to illustrate that they exercise an influence upon, and are in turn influenced by, the minister's appraisal, but also to represent the need for appraisal or assessment of these areas in their own right, through parish audit, deanery review, diocesan working parties, or, at national level, commissions studying detailed aspects of the Church's life and mission. I look at the way in which parishes might conduct a detailed assessment in Chapter 9. Although this book is concerned principally with individual appraisal, I shall not forget that ministry takes place in the context of the local, the area, the national and the universal Church. Appraisal will perhaps be one way in which the isolation of the individual can be alleviated and the remoteness of the centre challenged, so that all who minister in the Church, in whatever office, begin to feel they relate to each other as befits those who belong to the one Body of Christ.

Notes

1. M. Jacobs *Still Small Voice*. SPCK 1982, p. 39.
2. M. Taylor 'Theology and Collaborative Ministry'. *Collaborative Ministry*, Loughborough: CM Group, 1987.
3. ibid., p. 6.
4. ibid., p. 6.
5. ibid., p. 9.
6. ibid., p. 8.
7. For a further explanation of systems theory, see a companion volume in this series: S. Walrond-Skinner *Family Matters*. SPCK 1988.
8. *The Alternative Service Book 1980*, p. 356.
9. I owe this image and insight to Canon Tony Chesterman.
10. Private publication produced by the Department of Pastoral Studies, St John's Theological College, Nottingham.

TWO

Precedents and Parallels

If in some matters the Church tends to adopt a cautious attitude to possible changes and developments, it has begun to investigate the advantages and disadvantages of appraisal at least in parallel with, if not in advance of, some other professions. While industry and commerce have led the way in appraisal, followed by the Civil Service and a few other public services, for the most part appraisal has hitherto been done piecemeal in the fields of teaching (schools and universities), medicine, and other caring professions.[1] Nevertheless there are sufficient examples of appraisal, outside industry as well as in it, to make it possible to examine the questions and issues which might be pertinent to the promotion of good practice in the Church's ministry.

The example of commerce and industry, despite the obvious advantage of some years' experience in this field, does not present an obvious model for appraisal, since the aims of business organizations are clear-cut, being concerned essentially with making profits. There are also problems associated with appraisal generally. It is not necessarily as effective as it sometimes appears to be. Yet the difficulty of equating industry and the Church has not prevented some schemes for appraisal being adopted from the industrial or commercial model, as in one Anglican diocese where they recruited and briefed 'consultants . . . mainly from industry and public service voluntary organisations who possess the experience, skill and sympathy to help the clergy'. A different Anglican diocese adopted a Civil Service model when it first introduced appraisal. There are, however, many other types of organization, with a greater similarity to the Church, which have used forms of appraisal that provide pointers and indicate pitfalls in the application of such schemes to the ministry. In this chapter I shall concentrate on drawing out the most significant features of appraisal from a variety of professional and voluntary backgrounds. I particularly look at what are technically known as non-profit organizations or human service organizations, such as universities or youth and community services, since it is these which provide the Church with a better model than commerce and industry. This may, incidentally, reassure the reader who is concerned lest the Church simply wants to ape mammon and sacrifice effectiveness for efficiency. My aim is to identify the key concepts and questions which might need to be asked of any appraisal schemes within the Church, whether at the level of the diocese (or whatever title is given to a local area in other Churches) or in the local church. Such an analysis will provide a framework within which, in the next chapter, I can examine some examples of appraisal currently being used in different parts of church life.

What's in a name?

I have so far used the word 'appraisal', but it is only one of many such terms used to describe the process of examination or reflection. In alphabetical order, the alternatives include: assessment, audit, consultancy, evaluation, review, supervision and support.

In order to avoid subsequent confusion I will (except when directly quoting schemes or authors) use these terms in the following ways: 'appraisal' and 'assessment', although virtually interchangeable, carry slightly different connotations, the latter term suggesting 'marking' performance as in 'continuous assessment'. I prefer therefore to subsume both senses in the former, wider, and less evaluative term 'appraisal'. I use this to refer to the process of appraisal of the individual either by him- or herself, or by a second party or parties, who may be peers or superiors. It is concerned with past and present ministry as a whole, and takes a mid- to long-term view of future development and potentialities.

'Audit' and 'review' I likewise regard as being similar, but will use the term 'audit' in this chapter to include both senses; it is applied to the overview of the general purpose and achievements of an organization or group. This is the meaning of 'parish audit' as it appears in *Faith in the City*[2] (see Chapter 9). I shall also avoid using 'review' of this type of overview, since in some quarters (although not in this book) the phrase 'ministerial review' is preferred to 'appraisal'.[3] As will also be clear from this chapter, in some organizations 'review' is used as an alternative to the term 'appraisal' to indicate an individual activity. An 'audit' is more likely to describe what is actually taking place than to be a precise and detailed study of a piece of work or a project carried out by an organization. This more measured and more specific activity, which focuses on a more tightly defined area of work, I call 'evaluation'; this involves, for example, looking back at a project, evaluating its success and culling from its work information and understanding about its area of concern. I do not propose in this chapter to discuss evaluation in secular organizations, but in Chapters 7 and 9 I shall include some suggestions for evaluating local projects where there is a clear relationship to the type of activity in which some local churches may engage.

Both an audit, which is general, and an evaluation, which is specific, may give rise to recommendations for the future. Thus, putting these terms together, an audit which looks at ministry generally may lead to the recommendation that *appraisal* of individual ministers would be valuable. Once such a scheme has been tried (perhaps through a pilot project) it is possible and, I shall argue, also desirable that there should be at least an initial, and preferably a periodic, *evaluation* of the scheme. Of course, an evaluation may in turn lead to the recommendation of a further audit or evaluation of some aspect of church life or ministry.

'Supervision' and 'support' are again similar terms, although the former carries with it notions of the supervisor being in some way more experienced than the person being supervised. Yet peer supervision can also be effective, especially when it is informed by the methods and understanding such as are described in the companion volume in this series by John Foskett and David Lyall, *Helping the Helpers*.[4] Because support is only one aspect of supervision (which is also concerned with learning from situations) I use 'supervision' in this context to cover a formal or regular process of support and learning: meetings with a group of peers or an individual where the ministry of pastoral care, counselling or management of ongoing individual and group work is discussed, with a view to enhancing both practical skills, and pastoral understanding. The term 'support' I reserve for informal care and concern, such as an encouraging letter from a superior, or the interest and concern of the minister's partner or friends.

Thus a minister in *appraisal* may talk about her or his part-time ministry to a local hospital in general and appraise the use of her or his time there. In *supervision*, however, the minister is more likely to talk in detail about some of the pastoral relationships with patients or staff formed in hospital visiting and receive from and give *support* to her or his partner at the end of a busy day's ministry on the wards.

This leaves *consultancy* as again different for my purposes from either appraisal or supervision, although in some quarters it is used as a synonym for either. In this book I reserve consultancy for those occasions when an individual or an organization calls on a consultant, as someone with acknowledged expertise and experience of very particular areas of work, who can give advice or comment on a particular project or problem, usually (unlike supervision) on a one-off basis. So a minister may ask a medical consultant for technical information on the condition of one of his parishioners in order to understand better the medical factors to be borne in mind in pastoral care; or a consultant may be asked to comment on the dynamics of a staff meeting, especially if it is felt that something is obstructing good working relationships. Unlike an evaluation a consultancy is more concerned with commenting on the here-and-now and with a particular problem, and less with commenting on past successes or failures, although often a consultant will need to explore the past in order to understand better the current situation.

These terms, and the different ways they are used in the literature, make communication difficult. There are no standardized terms. If I labour these distinctions it is because the whole area of appraisal (and the other activities) is a complex one where the individual minister, local church groupings and the wider institutional Church intermingle in a potentially confusing way. Yet from this very complexity I have already begun to spell out a variety of ways in which appraisal and its equivalents can be used in ministry to benefit not just the individual minister but also his or her church, at different times and for different purposes, some of which I shall outline below. While it would be ridiculous for these processes to so dominate a minister's timetable that nothing else gets done (navel-gazing in the extreme!), ministry in a local church may include all the above forms of appraisal over a period of time, as in the following example.

The Revd Tom Thumb spend the first few months in his parish getting the measure of the people, his church and the area and working out some priorities for his ministry. While he was well *supported* by his wife at home and two good churchwardens in the local church, he recognized the need for *supervision* of his pastoral care and counselling work, and he found an experienced minister with whom he met once a fortnight for an hour to discuss in confidence some of the problem families with whom he worked. As a result of some of the matters that arose in supervision he also got to know a few other professional people who worked in the locality, whom he could contact as *consultants* on technical matters like Social Security entitlements or for a psychiatric opinion. An occasional phone call usually provided enough information, although once or twice a year he would meet one of his professional colleagues if a case was more complicated than usual.

After Tom had been in the parish for two years, he suggested to the church that they conduct a *audit* of church life and of the needs of the parish, to see whether there was a match between what the church was doing and what the community wanted. A small working party met several times, including meeting with a couple of Tom's contacts whom he used as *consultants* in order to benefit from professional advice. When the working party reported to the church council they recommended a drop-in centre for mothers and toddlers.

It so happened that about the time of their report and its acceptance by the council Tom had taken part in his first annual *appraisal*, a pilot scheme in the locality. Talking with his appraiser he had become aware of a tendency in himself to have to be involved in everything that was set up in the church; so he used the suggestion of a drop-in centre as an opportunity to let go the reins and allow a small group of mothers and toddlers to start the venture. He recommended a trial period of a year, getting someone from a neighbouring parish to *evaluate* the scheme after it had been going for six months. The evaluation showed that, despite some short-comings, the centre had begun to do some useful work and that some of the helpers needed and wanted assistance with their listening skills. Tom arranged for a local counsellor to run a short course for them and when it finished he himself met the helpers once a month to help them form a *peer supervision group*. At his second *appraisal* Tom was recommended to look at ways in which he could further his ministerial training; and he decided to take a short course in group-facilitating, as being likely to benefit not just this group of helpers but other work in the church as well.

This fictitious example demonstrates that the different forms of appraisal and evaluation did not take up an inordinate amount of Tom's time but helped him order his time better. By using various forms of appraisal at different times, Tom could benefit by becoming a more informed pastor. Other people could also gain from his willingness to monitor and evaluate what was going on in his own and the local church's ministry.

In this chapter I shall concentrate on *appraisal*, defined as an exercise in looking at an individual's ministry, as it is seen at work in a variety of organizations outside the Church.

What is the purpose of appraisal?

Many authors agree that if appraisal is to be introduced, one of the first questions that needs to be asked is, 'What is its purpose?' By drawing upon various studies of appraisal it is possible to identify very different objectives.[5] Randell et al. delineate four broad areas: reward reviews, performance reviews, potential reviews, and organizational reviews (they use 'review' as synonymous with appraisal). They say that studies of staff appraisal procedures often show that these purposes are not made explicit, and that indeed different objectives may sometimes be in conflict with each other.

1. Reward Reviews

a. Appraisal may look at the *past* performance of employees and whether they have achieved the goals set for them. As such it may be used to allocate promotions and 'perks' and to distribute bonuses or review salary levels, as well as to assist decisions about dismissals. Although it provides positive or negative feedback about levels of achievement, appraisal in these circumstances also becomes a process of control, serving the planning of an organization as much as, if not more than, the interests of staff—except those individuals who do well out of their appraisal. Clearly at any one time only a few can be rewarded, hence the necessity of the exercise. Furthermore a higher level of anxiety may be engendered in the individual when appraisal is of the reward type than when it is of the developmental type.

Brinkerhoff and Kanter, whose study of appraisal exposes some of the myths surrounding the claims made for it, set out this and many of the following aims; but they argue that an appraisal system should not be used either to make personnel decisions or to compile data centrally and that point 2(a) below (the developmental purpose of appraisal) is the most appropriate focus for an appraisal system. In this opinion they are supported by, amongst others, the Association of University Teachers (AUT), which has argued strongly against appraisal in universities being linked to promotion and awards, or to disciplinary action.

I draw upon the example of universities here partly to show that the idea of reward review need not be confined to commerce and industry, where profitability can be rewarded and shared, and that reward review in terms of promotion can take place in non-profit organizations. I also highlight universities because the position of academic staff and clergy is similar, both being paid and supported by a central institution, but both being employed to pursue work which is to some extent of their own choosing and highly individual.

The AUT states that 'part of the distinctive ethos of the university is the emphasis placed upon personal motivation, development and initiative', and this could be said to be just as true of the Church. Yet both academics and clergy have a responsibility not only to their chosen area of work but also to their employing authority.

An *AUT Bulletin* article warned against appraisal becoming a bureaucratic procedure 'governed not by the scheme's objective [to improve performance] but by its latent consequences, i.e. to use formal rules . . . to make performance *look* as good as possible'[6] (my italics). In preliminary discussions on a system of appraisal the AUT felt that appraisal was seen by the Committee of Vice-Chancellors and Principals as an additional tool for managing their institutions, and that the CVCP wanted to associate it with rewards and punishment. The AUT argued that improvement of efficiency in an institution would be achieved primarily through the particular staff who have management functions, and the development of their management skills, and that management criteria should not be put above individual development (see point 2(a) below). Nevertheless, the AUT Guidelines on the application of appraisal procedures accept that material emerging from appraisal might be used for promotion. Furthermore, one of the purposes for appraisal they agreed with the CVCP was to help identify and develop an individual's potential for promotion. But this was more to assist the individual in applying for promotion than to guide the institution in making its decision. Promotion reviews and appraisal had to be kept as separate procedures.

Likewise, while reward reviews as such are not immediately relevant to the Church, since salaries (or indeed promotion) do not depend upon productivity, the question needs to be asked as to how far some aspects of appraisal might or should be used for making appointments, especially senior appointments. Is it the case that any appraisal procedure conducted by a person who has the authority, influence or power to make or suggest appointments cannot help but contain an element of 'reward review'?

b. Appraisal may be used to set performance objectives. In some jobs these are related to financial reward, such as when a reward review not only looks at the degree of achievement of sales or productivity in the last year, but also uses these as a basis for production or sales targets for the coming year. Since those targets create markers for the allocation of rewards at the next annual appraisal, they can lead to feelings of being on a treadmill that goes faster and faster the harder people work. Performance objectives in this sense clearly reflect the demands of the organization even though, where they are met, they may also benefit the individual in financial or career terms.

c. Appraisal, according to Brinkerhoff and Kanter, forms part of the contractual bond between an organization and the individual, checking on the one hand that the individual complies with demands and that on the other he or she is protected against the arbitrary whims of authorities. Appraisal, for instance, provides employees with an opportunity to state their case for promotion or a salary increase, or to draw attention to any grievances concerning lack of recognition. Such protection is strengthened where there is machinery to enable an employee to appeal against decisions regarding, say, promotion or dismissal.

Trasler reports that the Institute for Personnel Management, in two surveys of companies in 1973 and 1977, detected a shift in emphasis from concentrating on past performance and linking this with salary increases, to greater concern for improving current work performance and assessing training and development needs. This is a change from what he calls the controlling function of appraisal to person-centred aspects. On the other hand, in a different sphere of activity, some research into appraisal (confusingly called 'supervision') in voluntary youth services[7] observes two distinct periods in the history of supervision in the youth service. The first, 1963-71, was a period of economic prosperity, where the emphasis was on the extension of training beyond college and the first professional post. The focus was on support and development of the individual, so supervision was non-managerial and consultative. The second period, 1980-87, was a harsher time economically, during which the emphasis was on management by objectives and on accountability. It may therefore be the case that in asking questions about the purpose of appraisal the economic climate, or the numbers game, influences the way in which it is conducted.

2. *Performance Reviews*

a. Appraisal can also perform a developmental function, concentrating more on the individual than the organization. Thus appraisal aims to help a person become more productive, efficient, effective or satisfied; this may be done by discussing and effecting training needs, by exposing inadequacies and deficiencies in skills which training might remedy. One company's set of appraisal objectives lists, in the following order, 'to identify individual development and training needs; to identify group training needs; and to identify individual strengths and talents to make full use of them.' A privately circulated local Probation Service document similarly stresses the purpose of appraisal as 'to stimulate and focus professional supervision on an officer's work, and to provide an opportunity to take stock of his development and to further it.'

b. Randell et al. acknowledge that punishment interviews may be necessary in management, but recommend a sharp reprimand at the time, when occasion demands; only if improvement fails to take place should this be taken up in a performance review. Performance reviews essentially dwell on the positive and on the blocks to positive growth.

c. Appraisal helps develop individuals by advice and information exchange, by coaching and direct training by the appraisers.

d. Randell et al. distinguish between the active and the passive performance review. Passive schemes simply try to maintain the initial level of interest in the work that has to be done. Active schemes add to people's inclination and capacity to work, trying to increase and develop their skill or knowledge to make them better at their job, and checking that the next developmental step is realistic. Thus another purpose is to stimulate the morale and motivation of the person being appraised to reach the standards and objectives of the organization through nurturing motivation. Randell et al. suggest that motivation to work is increased by identifying the brakes, blockages or frustrations which detract from a person's work. They believe that motivation comes from work that is satisfying. It is not that the right motivation makes work satisfying. In their words, motivation is 'derivative not causative'.

e. One company, progressively, in my view, includes one objective of appraisal as being to provide a basis for counselling and guidance.

f. A spin-off from appraisal may be that managers have to show their own accountability for the behaviour and effectiveness of their employees. Their performance as managers is in some sense being appraised by the very way in which they conduct the appraisal of those who work under them.

3. Potential Reviews

a. Indirectly, performance reviews may also assist a person's career development. The *AUT Bulletin* (September 1987) observed that the training department of Marks and Spencer, which allocates a considerable amount of time to staff appraisal, looks for areas of performance where improvement is possible and for future goals that are realistic. The AUT and CVCP agreed that appraisal should help staff to develop their careers within the institution and improve their performance. Randell et al. suggest that performance reviews include discovering the present and future work potential in both individuals and departments.

b. Appraisal can assist the allocation and management of human resources or justify personnel decisions. It may be used to construct succession plans, predicting the level and type of work which an individual might do in the future and fitting this in with the staffing needs of the organization. It also permits 'possibles' to see whether they really want to realize their potential by being trained and given special experience to prepare them for promotion. In industry senior managers are often seen as the best persons to conduct this type of appraisal, which requires experience, wisdom and managerial counselling skills, although Randell et al. still recommend training for this kind of work. Reports after such interviews need to be handled carefully, since it is unwise to raise expectations which cannot be met, especially if opportunities for high-fliers are few. One of a set of three appraisal forms used in one industrial concern states that this particular form is not to be shown to the individual being appraised because it includes potential for the future and, once seen, might be taken as a promise. Clearly this area is fraught with practical and ethical difficulties.

How preferments in the Church are decided is probably a mystery to most clergy and laity, although I doubt whether appraisal in the form of a potential review takes place as a stated procedure. Such appraisals for preferment are, I imagine, rarely discussed with the individuals concerned and tend to take place behind closed doors. But lest the idea of potential reviews appeals to those who wonder why they have been passed over for preferment, Randell and his fellow authors warn that this form of appraisal is 'the most dangerous in possible psychological effects, for statements about an individual's potential, or lack of it, can be psychologically disturbing.'[8] Not only are there difficulties in nominating 'crown princes', but the problem of how to identify and predict future human behaviour is one which taxes the whole area of occupational psychology. Nevertheless future planning within an organization is necessary, and training and special experience of possible candidates for preferment might, even in the Church, establish procedures that are more systematic than mere chance.

4. Organizational Reviews

a. Appraisal may be used, as the agreed advice for university staff appraisal suggests, to identify changes which might be necessary in an institution, if the organization is to help those who work within it to improve their performance.[9] Indirectly, therefore, individual appraisal may help improve the overall efficiency of an institution. In this case there needs to be feedback from individual appraisals to the institution, and a means whereby the organization is itself appraised.

b. Appraisal may again help the organization by more accurate assignment of work in relation to a person's abilities.

c. One company lists as an objective that appraisal also checks the effectiveness of employment interviews and selection.

While it is useful to distinguish between these four types of review and the different purposes for appraisal, it is also important not to isolate one feature from another. Several authors clearly place greater emphasis on the individual in appraisal than on the organization, although the former concern also serves the latter: 'If an organization is to be improved, emphasis, if not priority, should be given to attempting to improve the people who make it up. This is perhaps the key principle of human resources management.'[10]

In the end there is a close interrelationship, as a youth and community work booklet states,[11] between job development, personal development and organizational development. Similarly in the business world Randell et al. state that staff appraisal is 'aimed at improving the performance of the individual, the organization and the manager at their respective tasks'.[12] An AUT document refers to the improvement of a university as a whole, through development of the staff and through encouragement and support. The privately circulated local Probation Service document I have quoted already states similarly that the purpose of appraisal is to be of 'benefit to individual, to the manager, and to the organisation'. It succinctly summarizes the whole question of purpose with its observation that the benefit of appraisal to the organization will be the creation of closer working relationships, the highlighting of priorities, the identification of people with potential, the recognition of future training needs, and the harnessing of people's energies to the organization. This close relationship between the constituent parts and the whole is, of course, reflected in the Pauline image of the Church as a body where each member is a limb or organ of it. 'If one organ suffers, they all suffer together. If one flourishes, they all rejoice together.'[13]

Who conducts the appraisal?

While appraisal may initially be thought of (and in some quarters reacted against) as a hierarchical process conducted by immediate managers, or sometimes by even more senior staff, this is far from being an accurate picture. It may be true of commerce and industry, as well as of local government and the Civil Service, but Kilty delineates six basic arrangements for appraisal,[14] to which I have added further arrangements from other sources.

1. Self-appraisal by the individual alone. This ranges from a private and free-floating review, to self-appraisal using criteria that have been suggested by someone else; either form of self-appraisal might also be used as personal preparation for an interview with a manager or with peers, and as such may be written down and kept in the person's record, or used simply as an aide-mémoire.

2. One-sided appraisal of an individual by a manager, teacher or examiner, in which there is no comeback for the individual, who may not even know that such appraisal is being made or what criteria are being employed. Typical of such appraisal are private progress reports between more senior staff, references and, for students, examinations. Kilty says that this form of appraisal (he actually uses the term assessment, which tallies with my own feeling that the word carries connotations of external marking) tends to 'degenerate into oppressive, growth-inhibiting activities if the person assessing is immune from assessment himself or does not adequately sample competences or highlight strengths or is not open in principle to modifying his assessment in the light of the assessee's self-assessment'.[15]

3. Self-appraisal in the presence of another person, who is there to facilitate the process and to help a person to adhere to the self-assessment procedure. This type still concentrates upon self-appraisal but uses a second person to prevent self-delusion, excessive self-congratulation or even self-blame. Confronting questions may also be used to assist the subject's self-appraisal. This form may also be one part of a managerial or teacher's appraisal, in that the subject is given opportunities for self-appraisal even though other aspects of appraisal such as reports are also used. Self-appraisal using a second person can degenerate into ineffectiveness if the facilitator allows the assessee to lose his or her way, or to dwell on some aspects to the exclusion of others, such as strengths to the exclusion of weaknesses, or *vice versa*.

An example of the use of an appraiser as a sounding board in the context of a large organization seems to be developing in universities. Although the 1985 Jarratt report on universities recommended a hierarchical model of accountability, together with line management of academic resources, in working out an appraisal scheme,[16] it has been argued that academic staff should be allowed reasonable choice between reviewers, within a non-hierarchical system, with a second choice permitted if the initial appraiser proves unacceptable. It is suggested that it should not be assumed that departmental heads make the best appraisers; nor is it necessary for an appraiser to have detailed knowledge of the work of the person being appraised. Obviously in the academic setting (which, as I have suggested above, has some similarities with the Church) it is already recognized that peer appraisal may be the best way of achieving a relationship of trust and confidence between appraisers and appraised. In these circumstances, the person being appraised needs a choice of appraisers from a list of experienced and responsible members of staff, formally recognized by the institution as such, and both properly trained and given time for their appraisal duties. An appraiser may, but need not, be the head of department, as the next category would suggest.

4. Face-to-face appraisal with valid information about a person's performance. This is perhaps the most common

form of appraisal in large organizations, where there is the clear and deliberate intention to provide direct feedback from the assessor and to afford opportunities for both disclosure and suggestions about criteria and standards of work, as well as interpretations of the situation as reported by the subject and others. This arrangement can itself degenerate if it is not preceded by some form of self-assessment, if it is not conducted in a supportive manner or if the feelings of the assessee are ignored. Critical reflections will tend either to be ignored or to demoralize, unless some allowance is made for the assessee's reactions.

5. Self-appraisal in a group of peers, where the group may agree on the areas of competence which are under review and determine the criteria and the procedures for self-assessment. This form is equivalent to individual self-appraisal in a group context since the traffic is one-way: each individual reports her or his self-appraisal to the group; the group members hear it but do not make any appraisal of the individual themselves. The advantage of the group is that it determines the form which self-appraisal might take, and provides a supportive environment in which such self-appraisal can be presented.

6a. Appraisal of the appraisee by a group of peers who, in addition to listening to a person's self-report, may also share their own perceptions, doubts or questions about the person's report. Kilty cites the case-conference or supervision group as an example of this type of appraisal, but since I have already separated supervision out as a different activity, I prefer to reserve his category for peer group appraisal of work as a whole, or in a particular aspect, and not apply it to specific situations. It is equivalent to the facilitating, questioning and confronting of the two-person relationship outlined in the third type above.

   Kilty explores these last two types of group appraisal in some detail,[17] outlining about a dozen steps in the process of what he calls 'peer audit' (explained more fully in Chapter 7 below).

6b. Appraisal of an individual by a group who (though they may be peers) are put into a superior position because they form, say, an interview panel, a committee or tribunal investigating incidents or complaints, or even a committee or board discussing promotion in a person's absence. In group terms this is equivalent to the second type of appraisal in Kilty's list, where an individual is under scrutiny from others, but somewhat powerless (unless they are quick-witted enough to engage in any real dialogue with the panel), and where they may have little say in the actual decisions reached.

7. In addition to Kilty's list there is evidence of other means of appraisal. There is, for instance, appraisal by a person's subordinates, by a client group or by others who are affected by a person's work performance. Thus student feedback may be encouraged in schools and colleges. Those who attend courses are now well used to the 'evaluation sheet' handed out at the end. Travellers on package holidays are also familiar with consumer research. One industrial firm's appraisal form includes room for written reports on supervisors by those whom they supervise. Workers are asked for true/false answers to a number of statements such as 'He has on occasion led me to believe that he would do a certain thing, but has failed to carry it out', or 'When I know he is mistaken I feel free to tell him so and am not afraid he will resent it.' A different form of appraisal, more akin to this type of appraisal than to Kilty's professionally-orientated peer groups above, is 'co-worker evaluation', where an employee is asked to grade co-workers for such features as productivity, work approach, attitude, general intelligence and potential. In Civil Service appraisal, where it is conducted by the manager senior to the person's own manager, there is also an opportunity for the appraised person to comment on his or her manager, so that although appraisal is principally about the subject, information about line managers is gathered from the feedback of those who work for them.

8. Appraisal may also be conducted by someone from outside the work setting who is independent of the organization. Some companies use outside consultants from time to time,

particularly for 'head-hunting' and sometimes as part of the selection process. I have no evidence as to whether commerce and industry ever use outside appraisers or not, although I know of individuals who have chosen someone unconnected with their own organization as an appraiser or as a 'work-consultant'. If appraisal is primarily for the benefit of the individual, and since in any case it needs a skilled appraiser, it may be more important to use expertise from outside an organization than to rely on untrained or unpracticed appraisers from within it.

There are clearly some advantages in appraisal by an outside person since, as in the AUT's argument for a choice of appraisers in universities, talking with someone unconnected with managerial decisions may encourage that higher level of trust and openness which is necessary for honest and effective appraisal. There are, however, disadvantages in moving outside the managerial structures. An outside appraiser or a trusted and helpful colleague probably has no power and may have little influence to effect changes in the organization itself, if the need for them becomes apparent through the appraisal of the individual. Peer and outside appraisal also tends to disperse knowledge about an organization amongst different appraisers when it is gleaned through separate interviews, whereas line management appraisal allows knowledge to be brought together. Where trends are apparent and indicate the need for change in the organization, action can then be more readily taken. On the other hand, people may not always feel confident enough to make complaints about the organization to their managers (especially where the managers are perceived as having vested interests in the *status quo*). Randell et al., although they stress the value of the relationship between the manager and the person appraised, also observe that 'unfortunately most managers think that the relationship between them and their staff is better than it actually is.'[18]

In considering these different approaches to appraisal, it is unwise to make too hard and fast a distinction between the use of self-appraisal and appraisal by a second person or in a group. Self-appraisal is a useful tool before and after a more formal appraisal and may therefore be as much a part of formal appraisal as the main interview. Equally, even if a person is not required by his or her organization to present a formal account of her or his work to a superior, there are advantages in having the assistance of a second person for self-appraisal—someone who can gently challenge false assumptions and yet also provide some support through the exploration of the more stressful areas of a person's work.

What is appraised?

The task of appraisal is clearly, as a local Probation Service set of guidelines states, 'to review performance, not personality'. Nevertheless it is sometimes difficult, especially where personal qualities and professional skills complement each other, to see where performance and personality divide. This is clear from a number of forms of appraisal where personal qualities are either measured by means of rating scales or are explored through personal questions which require a written answer from the appraiser. For example, the following list of areas to be looked at, drawn from one appraisal form, includes headings that are not only to do with performance but also with the personal qualities that are necessary in the work: reliability, ability to get jobs done, personal standards, expression, knowledge of procedures, initiative, business sense, human relations, confidence, responsibility, contribution, progress, specific areas of knowledge. 'Reliability' is a good example of a term which looks at both performance and personality. In this particular form it is one of twelve headings to be graded on a scale of 1 to 4 with 'is entirely reliable in all aspects of the work' graded 4 and 'cannot be relied upon to do a job without supervision' graded 1 on the scale.

This type of appraisal form, scheduling in considerable detail the areas which the appraiser and appraised must work through, is very common, although the length of such forms varies. In some instances there are simpler guidelines set out for the appraiser, as is the case in a university annual review of administrative staff. Here the appraiser is asked to look at the following: responsibilities and duties that have changed since the last report; skills and qualities appropriate to present responsibilities; how far the staff member has developed in knowledge of the work; reliability, judgement, initiative, self-confidence, clarity of speech and writing and relations with others; and the interest he or she shows in extending the range of his or her work. As is the case in many forms of appraisal, the appraiser is asked both to record the advice given about areas where improvement is desirable and to comment on the potential of the staff member for advancement. In another appraisal system there is a separate form for comments about promotion which the subject does not see, although two other forms are countersigned as having been agreed by appraiser and appraised.

It would be tedious to summarize the many examples of appraisal which exist, although it is worth mentioning a few other areas under review which appear in the papers that have come my way. Some of them occur with considerable frequency and all of them may be relevant to thinking about appraisal in ministry: future training needs; relationships with colleagues and clients; response to supervision; the ability to work with, train and supervise volunteers; the development of subordinates; organization of own work; community involvement; response to stress and crisis; maturity of judgement; unused abilities; response to change and potential for future growth; problem areas; factors that prevent better performance; the most interesting task; the most successful area; areas of work where extra help is needed; the most difficult problems faced; priorities for the next year; and how the subject sees her or his future developing.

Valuable though some of these questions or guidelines may be in planning forms of appraisal for ministry, it is heartening, in the light of the paragraphs above and the account of procedures below, to read that Randell et al., who write from considerable experience of appraisal in industry, eschew any elaborate scheme, saying that a blank piece of paper is enough if the appraiser is a thorough and precise observer![19]

What procedures are adopted?

Brinkerhoff and Kanter observe that appraisal takes various forms, from official, formal meetings with an appraiser through to casual, chance, and informal observations and comments. Although it may at first appear that procedures are not necessary for self-appraisal, even in that case questions can be asked (the content) and a procedure set out, as a guide to the person appraising him- or herself. This may include reading through one's job description, deciding which parts of it to appraise, evaluating those aspects, and setting goals for the future.

That is a relatively simple form of appraisal. Trasler outlines two types of appraisal, objective and subjective. The objective is achieved through developing targets and criteria for measuring effectiveness. An example of such is described by Brinkerhoff and Kanter as having four components:

a. task allocation (clarifying the goals, which may include looking at the job description);
b. establishing criteria for accomplishment of goals;
c. sampling or measurement of the criteria (for example, the number of sales, or the number of papers published in a university department);
d. the appraisal itself.

Trasler observes that this type of objective appraisal is very difficult to do in some jobs and that it is also difficult to use fairly, since comparisons may be made on the basis of figures, without taking other variables into account. For example, salespersons in an economically depressed area may have far less opportunity to increase their sales over a given period than those working in rapidly expanding areas.

Then there are subjective methods which are very commonly used. Some methods of appraisal may at first sight seem 'objective' since various qualities can be rated through ticking boxes or scales or via graded statements. But there are difficulties about such an approach. Individual interviewers tend to score regularly in one of two ways: either centrally, towards the middle, or at one or other extreme, in neither case using the full extent of the scale. They also tend to be heavily influenced by recent performance. Their comments and 'observations' thus have a strongly subjective quality to them.

Actual procedures vary, although it is worth looking at two examples in detail. The first, from industry, involves considerable preparation time—a point which is worth noting since appraisal, if it is to be taken seriously, requires much more time than the interview alone. The person being appraised is asked to prepare for the interview by thinking about those things that prevent the job being done better—including lack of training, insufficient help from colleagues or poor management. He or she is asked to prepare a list of objectives for next year, together with areas that he or she wants to discuss with the manager.

In the meantime, three people (one direct superior and two others with whom the subject has dealings) are asked to complete a form and discuss their views with the person being appraised. These reports are collated by someone in the next senior level of management, who either discusses the reports with those who wrote them or moves straight to the interview stage. The reports are given to the subject early in the interview, if not in advance, and during the interview they are discussed. Appraiser and appraised try to agree mutually upon objectives, targets, key areas and performance improvement. The main points are then summarized in a way which is mutually acceptable. The manager keeps one copy of the summary, the appraised another, and a third copy is sent to the personnel department for decisions on training, promotions, demotions and transfers. The appraisal forms are kept for five years and then destroyed as no longer relevant.

While I do not suggest that this procedure is one which is applicable to the Church, it nevertheless indicates the thoroughness with which the task is approached. Universities, in discussions about the implementation of appraisal, can be seen to be taking equal care to ensure that the procedure is right and that it includes safeguards, even though the actual steps involved include some informal elements. We need to bear in mind that the procedures agreed for appraisal are based upon two objectives: the need for formal appraisal on behalf of the institution, and the need for an appraisal procedure which is aimed at improving personal performance for staff members. These two different objectives may also be present in some Church schemes for appraisal.

The procedure proposed for university staff starts with self-appraisal. Staff are given a self-appraisal form well before the date of their review to guide and structure their self-reflection, and to help them think about current plans, career development, training and support needs. There follows an informal private interview where the subject can speak freely, and where the appraiser gathers information for completion of the appraisal form. Finally the interview moves into a more formal section, so that agreement can be reached there and then about the information which is to be recorded and any follow-up action that is to be taken. The subject receives a draft of the completed form for comment and can suggest amendments. It includes space for him or her to comment on the conduct of the appraisal. This then becomes the final report. If there is any failure to agree on the record the subject and the appraiser meet again, inviting a third party to conciliate if they wish. If there is no agreement the subject can file a note of dissent. It can be seen that the person being appraised is involved at every stage of the process and that what is proposed is a two-part appraisal; the first part is free from the constraints of the final report and the second seeks to arrive at an agreeable way of formally recording the appraisal. Clearly the means is provided whereby anything particularly sensitive can be kept out of the final form, which both appraiser and appraised need to agree upon. The procedure for university appraisal also includes protecting the confidentiality of records. These are kept only by the reviewer, the subject and the head of department unless follow-up is necessary, or unless the report provides evidence for suitability for promotion, in which case just the relevant sections can be referred to. At regular intervals both parties review the records and destroy any that are no longer felt to be relevant. If a person changes appraiser, it is up to the subject to decide whether the records are shown to the new appraiser.

The combination of thoroughness and built-in machinery for safeguarding the interests of the person being appraised means that any worthwhile appraisal takes up considerable time and energy either side of the actual appraisal interview itself. This length of time limits the number of people one appraiser can see. Those who conduct appraisals have to fit this activity into all the other responsibilities involved in their work. Not surprisingly, the AUT recommends that no-one should appraise more than eight colleagues;[20] while in similar vein, in evidence from the commercial world, Marks and Spencer Training Department, we find the following guidance: 'To ensure that you do justice to your staff, you should ideally appraise no more than six members of staff per year.'[21]

The inclusion of instructions and guidance for the interviewer on a number of appraisal forms indicates that appraisal is not left to specialists. If it is to be done effectively and efficiently the task of conducting appraisals has to be spread evenly over a number of staff. Different guidelines stress the need to support, to use the strengths of the subject, to enable improvements to be achieved and to take action, as well as hints on how to conduct the interview. I need not dwell on those here, even though I do not want to neglect the obvious references to the training of appraisers which is evident in a number of places. I shall return to the question of training for appraisal of ministry in Chapter 6 and offer some guidance on conducting appraisal interviews.

Three further points need to be made about procedures on a general level, all of which are brief but very important. The first is that in some institutions (such as the Civil Service) appraisal means appraisal for everyone. When it was first introduced in the Civil Service, it was acknowledged that the proper place to start was at the top, so that no-one was permitted to conduct an appraisal until they had themselves been through the process. The AUT discussions have concluded that appraisal must apply to all categories of staff in universities, at all levels of seniority. The content of the appraisal may be different but the procedures are the same. There are obvious advantages in this, not least in terms of equality and fairness in providing appraisers with personal knowledge of what the experience feels like for the appraised. Nevertheless, in some organizations and institutions, appraisal is not required of all employees.

The second point is one which could easily be missed because I have come across only one reference to it in a vast amount of literature. It is the question as to whether appraisal is voluntary or not. The single reference (in Trasler) simply asks those who are considering introducing appraisal whether it is to be voluntary. All the other sources that I have consulted do not even pause to ask the question, although in the case of one organization an additional appraisal can be asked for over and above the compulsory procedure. This implicit assumption that appraisal is an accepted procedure is in itself interesting when part of the current debate in Church circles on appraisal is whether it should be voluntary or compulsory. Even in universities (where anything compulsory can easily suggest limitations on academic freedom) the discussion appears not to have been whether appraisal is compulsory or not, but how the welfare of the individual can be protected in the procedures that are to be adopted.

The third point again applies to the introduction of an appraisal scheme. There is some evidence that pilot schemes are favoured, before a full-blown scheme is applied to the whole institution or organization. 'All recent experience suggests that such pilot schemes are necessary to eliminate the problems inevitably thrown up when new procedures are introduced into complex organisations.'[22]

How often does appraisal take place?

Annual appraisal in industry is certainly the norm, but there are variations in other settings. A local Probation Service document sees appraisal as taking place initially after six months for a probationary officer, and thereafter every year for five years. After that appraisal takes place every two years until fifteen years' service, and then every three years. Senior officers, however, are appraised annually. Where officers ask for an additional appraisal, with a view to promotion, this consists of a full day's inspection of their work.

The widening interval between appraisals with increased length of service (though not, we note, with seniority) is reflected in one scheme in business where those between 30 and 40 who have been on one grade for three years and those over 40 are only assessed fully every third year, with an abbreviated form in intervening years unless such people request a full assessment.

Despite the normal frequency of appraisal being yearly, there are variations. In the youth service in particular there is one reference to the frequency initially being monthly for the first year and twice-yearly thereafter. It is not always clear whether the monthly meetings which are referred to in some of the literature[23] and called supervision, are any different from the definition I have given above, that is based on casework and application of skills within the work, rather than on the job itself. Yet monthly supervision appears to cover areas which I associate with appraisal, such as the work done under each section of the job description, areas giving difficulties, problems that need to be resolved, training needs, and so on; and biennial assessment is described as being about job skills, rather than the tasks related to the job.

In universities the suggestion is that appraisal takes place every two years, since greater frequency imposes too great a demand on time. There can, however, be interim reviews at shorter intervals if necessary.

What are the problems about appraisal?

Some problems associated with appraisal are common to particular forms of appraisal, others to the type of organization in which people work. It is also important to recognize that appraisal may in itself throw up further concerns, so that an organization might experience difficulties arising from the information gleaned from a number of individual appraisals. My comments are gathered from a variety of sources.

1. Difficulties in appraising

a. I have already referred to the subjective quality of some rating scales used in appraisal. There is a further subjective factor that needs to be added. Appraisers (especially where they have regular contact with the appraised) tend to remember the worker's best performance and most recent performance. The former is known as 'the halo effect', the latter as 'the recency effect'.

b. The use of lists of words, or choice of supplied phrases designed to prevent ambiguous value judgements, can also be limiting. It is difficult to categorize people in this simple way, especially when an appraisal is complicated (as it is likely to be) by some aspects of performance which are excellent and some which are poor.

c. It is not easy to observe performance (such as teachers in classrooms or pastors on home visits) without the observation itself detracting from the way a person normally works and behaves in that situation.

d. Where there is a diversity of levels of authority, one person may allocate tasks, another set criteria, another sample performance and another appraise. The accuracy of appraisal is then reduced. (This diversification of authority is typical of the Church, amongst other organizations.)

e. Although appraisal tends to rule out looking at personal qualities and concentrates more upon performance in trying to assess observable behaviour, it does not (quite deliberately) look at hidden personality traits. Yet it may be these that make all the difference between success and failure, or satisfaction and dissatisfaction with the work.

f. Brinkerhoff and Kanter suggest that powerless appraisers are less likely to use appraisal for developmental purposes, and may even use it punitively. This point needs to be qualified by other comments in the literature that portray managers as finding it very difficult to make confronting remarks or to be frank and 'constructively critical'.

g. Much depends upon the quality and training of the appraisers. All staff carrying out appraisals need to be adequately trained in the mechanics of it and in the objectives and operation of any appraisal system. This means regular training sessions to refresh skills. The 'establishment of a worthwhile scheme is dependent on a willingness in institutions to devote considerable staff time, energy and other resources to its operation'.[24] It is clear from a number of sources that the communication style of the interview is very important, with the right balance between positive and negative feedback.

h. Appraisal also depends upon its being shared and owned by the appraised person as well; it is a collaborative task, especially in setting tasks or goals. How far, given this relationship of trust and their agreement to participate, do those who are appraised have access to the data used in their appraisals? While openness is often assured, there may well be secret information which is never known; or personal private opinions may go on influencing an appraiser, especially where he or she has the power to allocate resources or to influence moves and promotion.

i. Appraisal also depends upon the right degree of frequency. Yet some organizations clearly do not provide enough time or resources to develop and put into practice a scheme which has any chance of effectiveness.

k. Because of the difficulties associated with appraisal, the monitoring and evaluation of any appraisal scheme is obviously important.

2. *Difficulties about appraising*

As I move from the examination of appraisal in secular organizations to an overview of appraisal schemes in ecclesiastical settings in the next chapter, a very important factor to bear in mind is that the Church cannot be equated with commercial or business operations where, for the most part, appraisal has been developed. I have deliberately introduced into this chapter information about appraisal schemes in other institutions, such as the universities or the Probation Service. At this point, where I introduce some of the difficulties about appraising, it is also essential to make a distinction between those organizations which are geared to making profits and those that are called non-profit organizations (NPOs), of which the Church is one. Although there are features about appraisal which are common to profit and non-profit making organizations, Brinkerhoff and Kanter say that non-profit organizations need a less elaborate system grounded in the realities of the task and the organization. They suggest that the more appraisal systems are asked to do, the less satisfying the results.[25] They also remark upon the trend in management theory towards human relations,[26] and upon a move towards the developmental functions of performance appraisal. It is this purpose for appraisal which is most suited to NPOs and may therefore be the one which most interests the Church.

Brinkerhoff and Kanter describe a number of characteristics of an organization's task that have an impact on appraisal and make it more difficult to effect. In all instances NPOs tend to show these characteristics:

a. Complexity. The more complex the task the more complex the appraisal needs to be, yet appraisal should essentially be kept simple. NPOs tend to have tasks that are complex, ill-defined and unpredictable. For this reason Brinkerhoff and Kanter say there is a special place for peer appraisal in NPOs.

b. Clarity. Tasks which are clear can be measured more easily. However, where goals are diffuse it is tempting to make tasks into goals. For example, one of an academic's tasks is to publish research, so it is tempting to appraise success in terms of numbers of publications; in the Church it might be tempting to measure success by the number of communicants, since providing services is an obvious ministerial task. One can measure attendance at meetings, but it is not easy to quantify a person's performance in the field of relationships. Furthermore, the goals of NPOs are dynamic, numerous, often inspirational, and as such they are in some sense also ambiguous.

c. Predictability. Unpredictable tasks do not allow accurate appraisals to be made. Where accuracy is difficult, other irrelevant factors tend to overinfluence an appraisal, such as the level of trust, social similarities and historical factors in the relationship between appraiser and appraised.

d. Interdependence. In NPOs, perhaps even more than in profit-making organizations, there is considerable inter-dependence between the people who work for them. It makes it more difficult to decide what each person contributes to the success or failure of the organization because they either work together or in an interlocking way. Their organization also tends to have close links with other organizations. NPOs tend to use volunteers who are not normally part of an appraisal scheme (although I can cite two examples of voluntary organizations where annual appraisal of volunteers does take place). NPOs are also accountable, not to shareholders but to those to whom they offer a service, though often there is resistance within an NPO to appraisal by the client group or by third-party funding bodies. Since performance is also affected by organizational structures, there is also the need to appraise the organization.

e. Authority. The hierarchical lines of authority in NPOs are few. Most appraisal systems work within a clear hierarchical system, with a fair balance between managers and managed. In NPOs management structures may be less substantial and in some cases even 'staffed' by volunteers, responsible for managing paid staff.

3. *Difficulties arising from appraisal*

a. Appraisal may sometimes be seen as a way of increasing staff performance and improving efficiency. Yet the problems may lie elsewhere and not in the performance of those who work for the organization. So, for example, when the AUT can say that appraisal does nothing 'to tackle the universities' real malaise, starvation of resources',[27] in the same way appraisal used in other settings may temporarily obscure other sorts of malaise. Different wings of the Church would no doubt argue that what is really needed is 'a return to the Catholic faith' or 'renewal by the Spirit'. While I share neither of these opinions, I would agree with the notion that appraisal, in itself, will not solve inherent institutional or personal problems.

b. At the same time appraisal is likely to expose difficulties in the institution which have previously been hidden. This may give rise on the one hand to the need for more resources, such as in the training and development of staff. However, staff development on its own does not necessarily solve problems. Negative comments about an institution can no more be brushed aside by suggesting more training courses, than can more training always be seen as the answer to an individual's difficulties. A youth service booklet comments that many of the problems experienced by employees, which are seen as appropriately treated in in-service training, actually stem from poor managerial supervision.

A report of a pilot project for an appraisal system in a local authority accounts finance department tells of requests for action and change in the structure and policies of the organization. Appraisal may mean exposing the more vulnerable parts of an institution or organization to criticism and necessarily thinking about change. It may, rather like the *lettres de cachet* before the French Revolution (the opportunity given by Louis XVI for letters of complaint), provide one of the pieces of tinder for a potential conflagration. It is for this reason that the highest level of management of an organization needs to take an active interest in appraisal, and has to be prepared to respond and show itself willing to consider change.

c. It has to be said, even though it may be an ultra-pessimistic view, that according to some critics appraisal in industry can be destructive and, by implication, counterproductive. Roy Oswald, quoting an American professor at a graduate business school, suggests a nightmare vision of what might arise from the wrong approach to appraisal:

> The basic fault of the annual appraisal is that it penalizes people for normal variations of a system. The merit rating nourishes short-term performance, annihilates long-term planning, builds fear, demolishes teamwork, nourishes rivalry and politics. It leaves people bitter, crushed, bruised, battered, desolate, despondent, dejected, feeling inferior, some even depressed, unfit for work for weeks after receipt of rating, unable to comprehend why they are inferior.[28]

d. On the other hand, appraisal, especially when it is sensitively conducted, may give individuals the opportunity to share personal stresses arising from their work, which hitherto they have not felt able to mention. This may in turn throw up questions about the care and welfare of those under stress. In the Church, therefore, there may be a greater need than ever for pastoral counselling services for ministers. In one great national institution, appraisal led to changes in outlook: more acceptance, for instance, that no-one could be good at everything and that it was legitimate to talk about weaknesses as well as strengths; but it also meant that ways had to be developed to help some of the staff to cope with matters that arose in their appraisal interviews.

Summary

In this chapter I have reviewed appraisal from a number of angles, drawing upon a sample of settings in which it already takes place, or where it is proposed in the near future. These provide us with examples of practice and help identify some key questions which I address in the next chapter, where a similar review can be made of appraisal as it is currently practised or proposed in different parts of the Church.

Notes

1. See, for example, for medicine: P. J. Sanazaro et al., 'Medical Audit'. *British Medical Journal* 1, 272, 1974 and 'Competence to Practice'. *British Medical Journal* 2, 1218, 1976; for schools: *Those having torches . . . teacher appraisal: a study*, HMSO/Suffolk Education Department 1985; for higher education: L. Elton, *Teaching in higher education: appraisal and training*, Kogan Page 1987.
2. *Faith in the City*. The Report of the Archbishop of Canterbury's Commission on Urban Priority Areas. Church House Publishing 1985. See Appendix A.
3. Canon Ian Hardaker uses the term 'ministerial review' in a number of papers privately circulated to Anglican bishops, recommending it as more acceptable than the term 'appraisal'.
4. J. Foskett and D. Lyall, *Helping the Helpers*. SPCK 1988.
5. In this and the following sections, I have drawn upon the following: D. W. Brinkerhoff and R. M. Kanter, *Formal Systems of Appraisal of*

Individual Performance: some considerations, critical issues and application to non-profit organizations, Institution for Social and Policy Studies, Yale University 1979; G. Randell, P. Packard and J. Slater, *Staff Appraisal,* Institute of Personnel Management, 3rd edit., 1984; J. Trasler, *Performance Appraisal,* The Council for Education and Training in Youth and Community Work (undated).

6. *Those having torches . . .* quoted in A. Waton, 'The Politics of Appraisal'. *AUT Bulletin,* September 1987, pp. 6—7.

7. A DES experimental project on supervision in the National Council for Voluntary Youth Services. *Briefings 2,* September 1987, published by West Central Counselling and Community Research.

8. Randell et al., *Staff Appraisal,* p. 24.

9. AUT/CVCP, *Career Development and Staff Appraisal Procedures for Academic and Academic Related Staff.* November 1987.

10. Randell et al., p. 11.

11. *Guidelines to a Staff Development Policy.* Leicester, In-Service Training and Education Panel (INSTEP) and Council for Education and Training in Youth and Community Work (CETYCW), 1985.

12. Randell et al., *Staff Appraisal,* p. 3.

13. 1 Cor. 12.14—26 (NEB)

14. J. Kilty, *Self and Peer Assessment.* Human Potential Research Project, University of Surrey 1978.

15. ibid., p. 5.

16. A. Jarratt, *Report of the Steering Committee for Efficiency Studies in Universities.* Committee of Vice-Chancellors and Principals.

17. J. Kilty, *Self and Peer Assessment,* and J. Kilty, *Self and Peer Assessment and Peer Audit.* Human Potential Research Project, University of Surrey 1979.

18. Randell et al., *Staff Appraisal,* p. 37.

19. ibid., p. 35.

20. *AUT Bulletin,* September 1987.

21. Marks and Spencer Training Department, *Appraisals.* Marks and Spencer plc 1987.

22. Association of University Teachers, *Guidance for Local Associations.* November 1987, p. 6.

23. *Guidelines,* and W. Feek, *The Way We Work.* Leicester, National Youth Bureau, 1982.

24. AUT/CVCP, *Career Development.*

25. Brinkerhoff and Kanter, *Formal Systems of Appraisal of Individual Performance,* p. 3.

26. ibid., p. 9.

27. *AUT Bulletin,* September 1987.

28. W. Edwards Deming of the Graduate School of Business Administration, New York University in an address entitled 'The Merit System: The Annual Appraisal — Destroyer of People', quoted by R. Oswald, 'Clergy Evaluation: a map of the minefield'. *Action Information,* The Alban Institute, Washington DC, 1988.

THREE

Principles and Practices

If appraisal sometimes seems just the latest bandwagon the Church is climbing upon, this belies the fact that different forms of appraisal and assessment (particularly the latter in theological training colleges and courses) have been developed over a number of years. Furthermore, as this chapter was being written, new information was flowing in at such a rate as to indicate that appraisal has been much more widely used than the current spate of experimental schemes would suggest. It is a complicated picture, to which it is impossible to do complete justice. But by trying to look at the picture as a whole and at some parts of it in detail, we can take the opportunity to learn from the variety of ideas and so evaluate our own particular method of conducting and participating in appraisal.

The beginnings of appraisal in ministry

It is probably to the Anglican theological colleges (and non-residential courses) that we must look for the first major developments of appraisal in the early 1980s. Since it was developed there in the context of training, to review academic progress and as a means also of making final recommendations for ordination at the end of training, there is that quality to it that merits the use of the term 'assessment' rather than simply appraisal. Assessment of students had always been made by staff without students being more than dimly aware that it was taking place, and they were unlikely to know what was being said of them in reports to the ordaining bishops. A few examples of the way in which assessment changed to involve staff and student will serve to demonstrate the openness with which assessment began to be approached.

The pre-ordination training course at Aston was one of the first to develop student participation. The Aston scheme reports have two purposes: the first educational, to help the student consider progress, the second to assess whether further training should be offered or taken up. Student and Principal write each other a series of detailed letters, in which self-assessment and comments are exchanged. Copies of these letters are then made available to the assessors, together with reports from local incumbents and pastoral tutors; these last are also made available to students. In addition to this 'public' assessment sent to the assessors and the sponsoring bishop, the Principal also conducts a personal and private assessment with each student which for some involves the discomfort and pain of looking at reasons for not proceeding to ordination training.

Similarly, assessment during and at the end of theological college or a ministerial training course influences decisions about ordination. This has put staff in powerful positions, especially when students have not been involved in the assessment process. An early example of change in theological college practice was at Ripon College, Cuddesdon, Oxford, where annual self-assessment became an open system. The tutor collected reports from different sources and discussed these with the student. Nothing was done behind a person's back. The final report was shared with the student, although even with student involvement we cannot forget that in the end the assessment was written by a staff member and was therefore a staff report. However, in a private paper written by one of the staff at the time this method of assessment was introduced, the comment is made that the relationship between staff and students changed slightly: 'The lines are clearer and slightly more formal, for now people are aware of assessment, whereas before they hardly knew it was happening.'[1] This process of discussion took place early and frequently enough (at least once a year) to be of use in training. It was not simply at the end of the course.

In addition the scheme involved student appraisal of the course and of the staff, and evaluation forms are now a feature of many training courses, be they term-long modules or day workshops. The Ripon College form allowed students space for comments on those who had supervised their academic and pastoral studies, space to reflect upon the year's course, and room to comment on the overall time allocated for different subjects.

Such developments have also taken place in ministerial training schemes (non-residential training). For example, the St Albans scheme involves a half-year profile, agreed by student and pastoral tutor, which is then passed to the course tutor; academic marks, comments from project tutors, support panels, incumbents and others are collated; and at a meeting between the student, the pastoral tutor and course tutors an agreed statement is produced as an end-of-year profile.

Such involvement of students in assessment is now universal in Anglican theological training and might be expected to set a precedent for future ministry, especially if assessment (and self-assessment or appraisal) is introduced not just as a hurdle to be jumped on the way to ordination, but as part of the ongoing development of ministry. There will always be some who regard assessment (like ongoing study) as one of those aspects of training which is applicable only to student life, to be left behind after ordination, as if that is when the 'real work' begins. Yet some of the forms of appraisal I have seen (especially one from the Pastoral Studies Department of St John's College Nottingham) could be extremely valuable to all ministers, at any stage of their ministry. The St John's booklet contains thirteen substantial sections for appraisal, including leading worship, group work, youth work, or evangelism; each of these contains a detailed and searching list of questions as an aid to reflection upon ministry.

Although post-ordination training was not one of the first areas to exploit the possibilities of appraisal, it deserves mention here as the natural place in which to pursue what has been begun in pre-ordination training. While there were (at least for Anglicans) formal methods of assessment such as 'priests' exams', there are signs of more exciting developments than purely monitoring ongoing academic progress. In places there are more open appraisals between training vicar and curate. In the Lichfield diocese, for example, the Board of Ministry developed a three-year system of appraisal for each curate and deacon(ess), to take place at the end of the first, second and third years after ordination. I include some details from it below, where I address the same questions to Church appraisal schemes as I did in the last chapter to secular organizations.

In addition to assessment in ordination training, much of the initiative for appraisal after ordination has come from those responsible for ongoing training in ministry called, in most Anglican dioceses, Continuing Ministerial Education Officers. They have often been involved in planning diocesan appraisal schemes and in the training of consultants; they have also been aware that appraisal will include an assessment of training needs and may therefore have a direct relationship to their own work. Diocesan Advisers in Pastoral Care and Counselling (where they exist) have also shown considerable interest in appraisal, especially in the process itself, in the resulting needs for clergy and their families which may be thrown up by individual appraisal, and in some cases in what individual appraisals may be saying about a diocese (or the Church's ministry) as a whole.

Anglican bishops who have taken the initiative for appraisal (which has often meant their own involvement in conducting it) have seen it as a way of getting to know many or all of their clergy in greater depth, and therefore as a potentially effective way of exercising their oversight and pastoral care of the clergy. One of the earliest and perhaps the best known diocesan scheme to date was introduced on a bishop's initiative. This was what has become known as 'Joint Work Consultation' in the Anglican Diocese of Liverpool.[2] Since JWC has had some influence upon the development of schemes in other dioceses, and certainly deserves special mention as a pioneering venture, I include further details of it under the various questions I address below. JWC was not, however, appraisal in the sense that reports were passed to the senior clergy. The difference became clear when in 1988 the Liverpool Diocese introduced an appraisal scheme *in addition* to JWC. Clergy are strongly urged to take part in JWC annually and in appraisal every three years. JWC is described in a diocesan report as 'task-related', whereas Performance Appraisal, as it is called, is 'individual-related'.

JWC is to do with setting realizable objectives in an area or areas of ministry on an annual basis; it is 'a form of in-house pastoral support to parish clergy emphasising the qualities of affirmation and confidentiality'.[3] Performance Appraisal is concerned with the direction of a person's ministry. And in this latter scheme (although this is not so with all appraisal schemes) an agreed report is sent to the bishop.

The reader will already have perceived an Anglican bias in the present description which owes its origins to more than the bias of the author. Although there is evidence of small-scale appraisal in other denominations, such as in the administrative headquarters of the United Reformed Church and an impressive scheme for the development of priests in many Catholic dioceses (looked at in greater detail in Chapter 4 below), it is the Anglican dioceses and sector ministries in Britain which have shown the most interest in appraisal. A number of surveys have been conducted of the developing patterns of appraisal in the dioceses of the Church of England. A 1983 report on sector ministries looked at the selection and appraisal of people for sector ministry (diocesan posts in mission, education, social responsibility, industry and commerce, etc.).[4] It found that 197 (over half) of the 367 posts were subject to regular appraisal, of which 40 were appraised by the diocesan bishop, 59 by the appropriate overseeing board or committee and 97 by others. Frequency of appraisal was mostly half-yearly or annual, though some replies indicated that it was as infrequent as every five years. Not included in that report were those ministering in the armed services and prison chaplaincies who also undergo the same form of appraisal as other personnel in their institutions.

In 1985 John Davey conducted a private survey of Anglican dioceses. He included 13 Roman Catholic dioceses, although my later description of the Ministry to Priests Programme means that I will avoid references to it in this chapter. He received 33 replies from the 43 Anglican dioceses. At that time six had no scheme for appraisal, one diocese had rejected it, twelve had it under review, and fourteen had an appraisal scheme in operation. It is not always clear what is meant in some of these replies; Davey lists some dioceses which claimed to operate appraisal, whereas my own knowledge of them suggests that what was available at the time could scarcely be described as appraisal in operation. Furthermore, what was claimed as appraisal in some other dioceses was a pastoral visit by the bishops to a parish, with every parish visited every three years or so. Valuable though such a visit may be, it essentially permits what one diocese (where such a scheme is in operation) calls a time of 'relaxed sharing' between bishop and priest. Such a time scarcely fulfils the requirements of appraisal, neither in its frequency, nor in its objectives or structure, nor in its informality.

The latest survey of appraisal schemes in Anglican dioceses available at the time of writing is a report prepared by Hiscox, Gammell and Raybould, presented for discussion in Anglican dioceses in June 1988.[5] The survey indicated that half of the dioceses had an appraisal scheme or were actively planning to have one but that only a third had a scheme in operation at that point. As might be expected with such a rapidly developing idea, the information on the number and types of diocesan schemes was out of date before it was published, with some dioceses recorded as having schemes when they were no longer in existence, while in other dioceses schemes had been introduced. Much seems to depend on the attitude of the diocesan bishop, and where changes of bishops have occurred so too have changes in appraisal schemes. I take it as axiomatic that where there is an appraisal system in operation, bishops and their staffs should be appraised as well.

The variety of approaches in dioceses, as well as the changes that may take place when there is new leadership, make it difficult to maintain continuity of ministerial appraisal and development within dioceses and also as clergy move from one diocese to another. Yet if appraisal is to be part of the long-term development of ministry, continuity of frequency, style and responsibility is essential. However jealously guarded the independence of dioceses and, in the non-conformist tradition, of local churches may be, in some aspects of ministerial development a more universal approach could be beneficial. To move from one method of appraisal to another when changing dioceses will require a period of adjustment; once a particular method and set of questions has been accepted, it is easier to use the same form each time. To move from a diocese with a compulsory system to one with a voluntary system, or *vice versa*, leads to potentially invidious comparisons. But if any assessment of clergy is to be made at all, drawing upon their appraisal or their self-appraisal, the only fair comparison between them has to be based upon the same tools for assessing them. Otherwise the more thorough system puts someone at an unfair advantage or disadvantage.

Names

In the last chapter I set out the way in which I was going to use the possible terms for appraisal in the context of this book. When we come to examine those in use in present schemes, the confusion of terms becomes obvious. Liverpool Diocese called its initial scheme 'Joint Work Consultation', and 'Work consultancy' has become popular in some quarters as a title for appraisal itself, although, as already stated, Liverpool Diocese now has an appraisal scheme which is different from work consultancy. However, in an important document which has influenced several dioceses in the introduction of appraisal Canon Ian Hardaker draws a distinction between appraisal and consultation, believing this to be necessary 'if much initial suspicion and opposition is to be dispelled.'[6] For him consultation is equivalent to counselling or spiritual direction and is more concerned with inner being.

Appraisal appears to be the most widely used term, although assessment and evaluation as well as development review also appear. Although I have chosen to use 'appraisal', the report by Hiscox et al. suggests 'ministerial review' as a more neutral and therefore more acceptable expression. In the end, of course, what makes a scheme acceptable is not its name but the way it is both conducted and followed through.

The purpose of appraisal

Using the different purposes of appraisal outlined in the last chapter, there emerges from various reports a similar picture of the stated aims in dioceses and other organizations. Using old reports in this way may lead to false impressions about the views in particular dioceses now, so I omit references. What is more important than academic accuracy of reference at this point is the way in which appraisal has been and currently is seen by those who have been responsible for its introduction.

1. Appraisal as serving the organization

Assessment during and at the end of training, which results in decisions about the suitability of a person for ordination and about his or her appointment to a particular place, clearly serves the Church as a whole as well as the individual concerned. Given the difficulties the Church has in pruning its 'dead wood' later in ministry, it is important that correct decisions are made at the start, both in selection for training and recommendation for ordination at the end of training.

Appraisal during ministry itself also is seen as serving the institution. The following quotations illustrate this aspect:

— It enables the more effective deployment of the clergy through a reliable assessment of a person's abilities and potential and the requirements of particular jobs;
— to enable the Church to develop a wide range of ministry in which the individual may play a full part;
— to help solve some difficulties over appointments by providing reliable knowledge about a man's [sic] ministry; to provide an opportunity for the bishop to have an objective way of ensuring, as far as possible, that suitable appointments are made;
— does the Church have clear goals—or, on a lower level, does the diocese? For, if work is being evaluated, there should be some standard against which to evaluate it;
— for the more effective conduct of the Church's mission; to identify the aims of the organization in which a person works.

The last is a particular reference to sector ministry, to ensure that such posts contribute to the policy of the appropriate board and of the diocese.

These statements are not, of course, made in isolation from

other aspects of appraisal, even though they illustrate the way in which it might be used, particularly when conducted by senior staff. The purposes which follow considerably enhance the total picture, but it is worth quoting by contrast: 'The primary purpose of appraisal is not promotion potential' but 'to assess the ministry of the whole Church in an area and therefore the combined ministry of priest and people.'

2. Appraisal as serving the individual

The most commonly stated aim of appraisal is to support and develop the minister. This is seen in a variety of statements, which describes the purpose of appraisal as follows:

— affirming the particular gifts of the curate/deaconess (from a post-ordination scheme);
— to identify a priest's abilities and potential growth points as distinct from his personal spiritual development; for the clearer understanding and definition of the role of the priest in his setting, so that he and others can have realistic expectations and criteria by which he can appraise his work;
— for the setting of achievable short-term objectives in a man's ministry;
— to help you resolve any difficulties which affect [your] ministry;
— they [the clergy] can talk freely and confidentially about opportunities and frustrations, relationships in the parish, particularly when they are difficult, and the way in which they can use their time and skills to the best advantage; to enable our staff to develop as people and in their working skills during their time with us.[7]

3. Appraisal as pastoral care

When appraisal is either conducted or promoted by a bishop and his staff, it may be seen as a means of control; but a different motive for appraisal is also put forward by senior clergy which demonstrates the pastoral rather than the managerial aspect of the episcopal (or equivalent) role.

Appraisal is seen as one way of enabling the bishop to exercise his proper care for his clergy. Thus appraisal is described as follows:

— pastoral concern (by the bishop) for the minister and his work;
— the building up of mutual confidence and trust between the priest and those with whom he shares responsibility for his work (bishop, archdeacons, colleagues, lay people); the provision of thorough and sensitive pastoral care and support grounded in a surer knowledge of the clergy and their families;
— a scheme for lateral caring and mutual support by members of the Body of Christ for one another.

The last phrase comes in the context of a bishop's address to his diocesan synod, in which he describes appraisal as a means whereby clergy can have a more immediate guide and counsellor than the bishop, who cannot perform this function realistically 'to so many people over so wide an area in such a variety of situations'. In fact a slightly different emphasis is given to care of the clergy here, because the bishop goes on to say that 'it is an inappropriate model whereby every minister looks to father either to tell him what to do or to solve his problems, or to be the object of unreasonable hates, disappointments and dependence when either he fails to perform these tasks or performs them in a way which runs contrary to the individual's desires.'

Whether appraisal itself is the most effective way of exercising care of clergy is a question which needs to be raised. It may be that there are other paths, less formalized and less open to suspicion, which provide openings for clergy to share their concerns, personal and professional, in their ministry.

4. Appraisal of past performance

Strikingly absent from descriptions of appraisal in the Church setting is any reference to past performance, perhaps because this aspect of appraisal in secular organizations is less immediately quantifiable in the context of a pastoral ministry.

The closest reference is a suggestion about appraisal in sector ministry: that it serves to modify job descriptions. Clearly this involves looking at what the past year has shown to be manageable or not manageable in respect of the existing job description. Generally there is a refreshing absence of requests for statistics! Many appraisal schemes seem designed for the first interview only; but ongoing and regular appraisal must surely question how far previously set objectives have been met or previously mentioned difficulties resolved. An obvious exception to this is seen in the appraisal used in an Industrial Mission, where each year the person sets out personal objectives in relationship to the overall aims of the Mission, accompanied by criteria for success. During appraisal last year's objectives are reviewed, and the reasons for success or failure to meet them are identified.

5. *Appraisal for future development*

Much more frequent are references to development and the way in which appraisal assists future planning. Joint Work Consultation, for example, is described as an activity 'in which they [the clergy] try to look at what their calling is, to get some objectives for the next year and to review how it's all going.'[8] Other references elsewhere include as examples of this purpose of appraisal:

— to discuss priorities for the coming two years;
— to discuss how your ministry may be developed through further opportunities of training, additional support, move to new responsibilities, etc.;
— to identify training needs;
— to prepare the clergy and laity for their appropriate roles today and tomorrow.

6. *Appraisal for promotion or reward*

While this purpose is linked to 'appraisal as serving the organization' (above), I include this as a separate heading to emphasize an aspect of appraisal which is more evident in the secular world than in the Church, perhaps because there

are generally more openings for promotion and more opportunities for financial reward in secular than in ecclesiastical
institutions. It is therefore not surprising that there is little
reference to these aspects of appraisal in the literature from
the churches, except one reference to formal appraisal as
existing partly to identify people's movements, including 'high-
fliers'. However, there is no obvious suggestion here that so-
called high-fliers might be cultivated and trained, so that
their career development is nurtured with specific help both
in preparing them and in testing their suitability and their
response to greater responsibility. Given the reference in the
previous chapter to the need to avoid identifying 'crown
princes' for their own good, perhaps the same need is felt in
the churches!

The other side of promotion and reward is the more
negative one (which is also part of secular appraisal) where
annual appraisal results in standing still, moves sideways,
demotion or even dismissal. Again there is no obvious
reference to this in the Church literature, and it may be an
area which cannot be mentioned when trying to promote the
positive features of an appraisal scheme. One proposal
mentions the need to provide support for those who are not
making the grade in a certain area of their work, which may
involve training or changes in working patterns. This side to
appraisal raises issues about the resources available to those
who for one reason or another are not effective ministers. It is
one thing to provide training and advancement for those
whose talents are obvious; it is another to ensure not only
proper support but also the right work setting for those
whose ministry is at worst ineffective and dead, or at best
slipping into negativity and despair. The need for more drastic
action remains a problem for the Church, although with the
attempts to end tenure in universities, the Church and
perhaps the senior echelons of the Civil Service are fast
becoming the only places where jobs are held for life and can
only be lost as a result of immoral conduct.

Models of appraisal

The Church has had to use the experience of appraisal in

secular settings and in doing so has adopted models from a variety of institutions. One diocese has drawn on a system used by a county council, another on that used in the Civil Service. Joint Work Consultation in the Liverpool Diocese (influential in itself because of other dioceses following Liverpool's lead) borrows 'insights from the world of business and commerce'.[9] Certainly the identification in JWC of measurable areas for appraisal seems to be consistent with such an influence.

The problem with borrowing from the secular world is that such institutions can be regarded with suspicion by some clergy. In part this may be because industry is felt by some to represent the worst features of mammon, although there is also the more down-to-earth consideration that a commercial organization cannot be equated with one which is concerned with sacrificial giving and the power of redeeming love. Some clergy may feel that the Church cannot be run like a business and that appraisal smacks too much of cost-effectiveness and profit-making. My own inclination towards this view is seen in my distinction in the last chapter between organizations that exist to make profit and those which exist to serve human need. However, efficient use of time and resources is common to both, and yet some ministers are equally suspicious (perhaps with good reason) of making a god of efficiency. And even those who argue that the Churches need to be far more business-like in their management observe that this is difficult when senior clergy and their staff are not trained in the methods and organization used in the business world.[10]

Who appraises?

The Hiscox report includes a chart with four methods of appraisal, distinguished by who it is who conducts it, each with its own emphasis, way of reporting, advantages and disadvantages. In fact there is an even greater variety of practice than this, although I list first (in a different order) their four methods, with a description of each type.

1. *Individual self-appraisal*

There is little reference in the literature to this form of appraisal. One church youth service writes that 'all full time workers are required to plan their work, and to self assess themselves. A written copy is required to be sent to national headquarters every month.' Hiscox et al. observe that this is the least threatening method and easy to offer to all, but it lacks outside support and care and does not encourage commitment to action or clarify training needs. No information gets passed to those who have influence unless the individual takes the initiative.

2. *Self-appraisal using the help of a 'consultant'*

In this instance the consultant is non-managerial, perhaps a peer, but more likely to be a more experienced colleague within the diocese. In some dioceses there is a list of consultants available; in one diocese half of these are lay people, while in another nearly all are laity familiar with conducting appraisal in their own sphere of work and possessing the necessary experience, skill and sympathy. One diocese stresses that it is better to see an 'impersonal adviser' rather than a personal friend, although another suggests checking one's self-appraisal with a close friend before meeting a consultant. A different diocese stresses that the consultant should not be in a hierarchical relationship, thus distinguishing this method of appraisal from the one that follows. Hiscox et al. stress the need for confidentiality in this approach but also point out that an outside person enables a frank, clear, and challenging discussion to take place. Its weakness is that there may be less commitment to action, and that there is less likelihood of information being passed to those in authority, unless special steps are taken by the individual.

3. *Hierarchical appraisal*

Although hierarchical appraisal happens in a limited number of places, it is rarely of the management type. Instead there is a tendency to use hierarchical structures as a convenient way to implement an appraisal scheme. Thus in one diocese rural deans may be consultants but not normally in their own deaneries. In the Liverpool Joint Work Consultation each person speaks to the person next in line: incumbents with area deans, area deans with archdeacons, and so on, although with the advent of a separate appraisal scheme, the intention appears to be that area deans conduct the appraisal and 'colleague consultants' the more confidential Joint Work Consultation. Appraisal in that diocese is much closer to the hierarchical model, with the bishop expecting all who hold his licence to take part in both appraisal and JWC.

Rural and area deans are sometimes mentioned in the planning stages of appraisal schemes as representing a type of middle management, which allows for a better ratio of consultants to clergy than can be managed when a bishop's staff alone is used. Following the lead of the commercial world, it certainly seems undesirable that a consultant should see more than ten to a dozen people for annual appraisal. Clearly such a favourable ratio is beyond the scope of present church hierarchies, which provide little place for an effective middle tier of management.

Given the problems of either a bishop or his staff seeing their clergy every year (it has already been stated that appraisal is a time-consuming process) a compromise is sometimes reached whereby in one diocese, for example, the bishop will see the clergy once every three years, but in between times they have a list of consultants to choose from so that they can arrange their own self-appraisal. At least two Anglican dioceses are now using both compulsory managerial appraisal and voluntary work consultancy, only the latter being annual.

In fact few Anglican dioceses have chosen managerial appraisal where detailed reports are written, passed to the bishop, and kept on file. Research for the Hiscox report found four such dioceses, although the value of their information is dubious, given some of the misleading replies they received. That report lists the following advantages of the hierarchical method: there is more commitment to action; the bishop has more up-to-date information about the minister and parishes; and the minister feels more cared for by the bishop. Against this, the report suggests disadvantages to this approach: it is more threatening; people feel they are being inspected and this method may lead to less honesty; it is difficult for senior staff to handle authority and care at the same time; and such an approach may lead to unrealistic expectations about future appointments.

Churches and Christian organizations also employ a number of people in an administrative capacity. Where line management structures are clearer, there is more evidence of managerial appraisal. For example, to quote from a large and then a smaller church youth organization:

— Both managerial and non-managerial systems of super-vision operate within our youth service. The national training scheme promotes the inclusion of non-managerial supervision in the support networks and structures provided for youth officers;
— All staff have line managers, the quality of supervision does vary.

4. *By peer group*

The fourth method referred to in the Hiscox report is that of group appraisal. Although I have referred to this approach in the previous chapter and will look at it in greater detail in Chapter 7, I find no evidence so far for its use in church settings. Hiscox et al. recommend it as providing continuing support and insights from a variety of points of view, but list more disadvantages than advantages: such a method is likely to degenerate into general discussion; it is more difficult to challenge individuals in a group setting; there is less commitment to action planning; and it is difficult to set up and sustain this pattern. Despite all the difficulties there are in getting clergy to work co-operatively, there may be room for such an approach where clergy are already working in teams, perhaps to supplement individual appraisal and to concentrate on the individual's work within the team or group itself.

5. *Outside consultant*

I include this approach separately to indicate the potential value of a work consultant who is either outside the Church altogether or outside the administrative unit (e.g. diocese or district) in which a person has employment. I also highlight this method for those whose work bridges two or more spheres of influence. So, to quote a church organization: 'A number of our local churches employ youth workers. Such matters as these [i.e. appraisal] are the responsibility of the local church. We would however encourage youth workers to slot into the relevant procedures in their LEA.'

6. *By the 'consumer'*

Thankfully the person in the pew, or the people whom ministry serves, are not forgotten in the desire for professional improvement, although there is less evidence than one would like of the views of the 'consumer' being taken into account. One post-ordination scheme envisages that not just the training incumbent, but also the tutor and one or two members of the congregation should be included in the process. Similarly, in the Greater Manchester Industrial Mission appraisal involves meeting a main appraisal group of one clergy and two laity at least three times annually for up to two hours; over and above this the chaplain to be appraised convenes a local group of representative people from major sectors of his or her work, which meets first on its own and then with the main group.

'Consumer' opinion is equally important when there is major research into ministry and mission. I give examples of this in a parish setting in Chapter 9, although the most thorough investigation of an area of ministry which I have seen involved not only the 'consumer' but colleagues as well. The research was made necessary by the need to demonstrate the efficacy of hospital chaplaincies in the USA. The chaplains themselves felt that the people who should evaluate their work were, in descending order, other chaplains, patients, nurses, other staff, patients' families and physicians. Instruments were produced for each of these categories to

assist the evaluation, with appropriately different questions
in each set of instruments: e.g. physicians were not asked,
although all other categories were, whether the chaplain took
the spiritual needs of the other person seriously; only other
chaplains were asked whether the chaplain viewed prayer as
a vital part of his or her ministry; only patients were asked
whether the chaplain listened to their feelings about their
condition. It is useful to note the sensitivity of this approach
in not asking people to make statements about areas about
which they probably had little knowledge.[11]

The content of appraisal

As is to be expected, the content of appraisal as set out on
paper varies from the (deliberately?) vague to the most
detailed questions. One diocese, for instance, suggests no
fixed agenda, but rather that the consultant and priest should
meet to talk about the agenda and so set it out for future
meetings. At the other extreme are the detailed questions
asked in the Liverpool Joint Work Consultancy.

In JWC the emphasis is on a person's work and not on
their spiritual life. Possible areas for discussion are worship,
evangelism, education, administration, finance, pastoral work,
ecumenical activities, social and community involvement,
family life and personal development and theology. The
purpose of appraisal is to identify aims and objectives that
are realistic, verifiable and obtainable.

Nevertheless, the suggested list of topics is not intended as
a set agenda for each appraisal. It is important to recognize
that attention can only be given to a small number of aspects,
which are to be chosen by the person being appraised. One of
the authors of the scheme comments:

> The restriction . . . to a relatively small number of job
> aspects is justified on three counts; first because experience
> in business suggests that a relatively small proportion of
> job activities produces the most important and significant
> results from that job; therefore second, because such a
> restriction forces a consideration of the key result areas of
> the job; third because it makes possible and practical an
> allocation of priority.[12]

The choice of topics depends on the needs of the situation, that is the needs of the parish, and on which aspects of the job have the most impact and are therefore to be given priority.

By concentrating on these relatively few aspects a minister can see what progress is currently being achieved in them, and can then express that progress in measurable terms, which then enable any further progress to be recognized and verified. Here the strong influence of business appraisal is apparent. An explanatory booklet gives some examples of the type of questions which permit measurement. In 'education', one of the three work areas which are examined in detail, the checklist of achievable aims includes questions such as 'have you a list of all engaged in education work in the life of your congregation? Do you have a list of members of your congregation who are professional teachers? Do you call at the schools of your parish from time to time regularly?' But while certain questions permit a quantifiable answer, others do not, although they are none the less particular. In the section on 'theology', for example, a quantifiable answer can be given to the suggestion of recording for a month the time given to the Bible, newspapers and any other book requiring a mental effort. But other questions are less precise, such as one which asks, 'Do we answer the personal problems of our people . . . by reference to our theology or to expediency or even to commonsense?'

Such checklists are not uncommon in appraisal schemes and can be of value both in preparation for appraisal and for the person who is conducting the appraisal. In JWC these 'explorations', as they are called, were written by people with expertise in a particular field and so 'provide authoritative guidance and guidelines'.[13] Each area has a standard format: definition of the area being explored; value judgement of the importance of the area; relationships with other areas of ministry; problems typically encountered; support from Scripture; a possible audit framework; a list of activities included within the area; and illustrations of the potential of this area for attention.

Like JWC, the brief study of appraisal in the report on sector ministry suggests the need for deciding clear objectives.[14]

A fictitious example is given there of Miss Jones, an RE adviser, who has as one of her tasks advising church schools on the curriculum, resources and classroom practice. The report suggests that appraisal should result in developing clear objectives for action, such as arranging a residential course. Such detailed planning is not built into every appraisal scheme and where it is, there is a clear need for at least an annual meeting to keep up with progress in meeting objectives.

Measurement scales are rare in church appraisal schemes, although I have seen four examples of them. Two were from the services and prison chaplaincy, where appraisal takes a standard form used with all staff in the institution; a third was for private confidential use by the interviewer when reporting back to a bishop's staff (a hierarchical scheme), and the fourth is the specimen form suggested for use in self-appraisal in the report on Sector Ministry. Here a 0 to 8 scale is used to rate the different levels of interest, effort, clarity of objectives, confidence and coping both twelve months ago and now; it is also used to rate skills, or what pass for skills, although they seem more like personal qualities (such as 'willingness to review new ideas'). In this case, where the score is less than it was twelve months before, this might suggest cause for concern, the time to look at what might have gone wrong and at the possibility of a move.

Some forms of appraisal include what I can only call 'weighty' questions, which might call for considerable time and attention. One ecclesiastical area asks for detailed information about the parish itself, as well as the significant changes in parish, congregation and personal life that have taken place in the last year. Others in the same form are quite complex: 'What do you personally perceive as the main functions of the ministry to which you were ordained? In what ways have these views developed from your earlier thinking as a result of the work you now do?' Yet another question addresses the policy of the diocese and its priorities.

If there is one area for appraisal which is liable to cause concern, it is that of the personal, spiritual and domestic life of the minister. In fact there is every indication that these aspects are included in many of the examples of agendas for appraisal. In one questionnaire, to be completed prior to a bishop's visitation, there are questions about the time spent in prayer, worship and Bible reading, as well as time off. But the tone for reflection on such personal matters is set well before ordination in college and course assessments. One ministerial training scheme, in addition to academic issues, looks at family, spiritual and other personal factors. The Aston scheme assessment is concerned not only with educational development, but also with personal maturity, spiritual growth, relationships with others, and what is called 'teachability and stickability'. A theological college form of self-assessment lists topics such as 'How I see myself' and 'How others see me', leadership qualities, 'How I respond to criticism and praise', as well as questions about spirituality, patterns of worship, and meditation. A diocesan scheme for the newly ordained includes headings about personal gifts and qualities, pastoral gifts, and personal and group relationships.

Whatever reservations one may have about the inclusion of personal matters in job appraisal, there is no getting away from it. The headings and questions point time and again to these areas, as well as to family matters, working wives, children and schooling, aged parents, etc. Even Ian Hardaker's suggested agenda includes topics such as whether wife and family are receiving enough of the minister's time, despite his concern to separate appraisal from consultancy, the former to look at work, the latter at a person's inner life.

Reports from more central sources suggest that such personal areas cannot be left out of ministerial development as a whole. An ACCM memorandum in 1980 suggested that assessment after and during training for ministry should include personal growth and development as an important part of a ministerial formation, and that assessment of this means crossing 'a major educational threshold' requiring the development of particular skills. The report on sector ministry suggests in its guidelines for conducting appraisal interviews that emotional issues should be allowed to emerge: 'Feelings and attitudes are closely bound up with effective job performance.'[15]

Procedures for appraisal

Since appraisal is so new to the majority of clergy and other church ministers, there are a number of examples where a diocese starts with a pilot scheme:— sometimes in a deanery, sometimes with those in sector ministry, sometimes with selected clergy who will respond favourably to a 'trial run'. In at least one instance there has been an organized time of preparation for the clergy being appraised, through workshops, as well as training for those who will do the appraising. But appraisal as it is presently conducted normally starts with a list of questions for personal consideration. In some instances this self-appraisal is written and may be accompanied by other written information, such as peer group assessment, feedback from laity, parish magazines and other relevant literature. The form can sometimes be very detailed, perhaps with room for full descriptions of the parish, and the ministry within the parish.

There is little information on the setting of the interviews, although in Liverpool JWC the rural deans take the initiative in preparing incumbents and in ensuring that the details of JWC are mutually acceptable: the day, date, time and duration and location. There are a number of examples where those conducting the appraisal are recommended to undergo their own first, and this may be made known to the clergy too. In JWC rural deans are recommended to have their own consultancy with an archdeacon. In another diocese the bishop makes it clear that he and his staff have consultants for their own appraisal, commenting upon his own experience that he had had his 'eyes opened about the possibilities for good in such an exercise. Previously I should have been pretty sceptical.'

Where appraisal is conducted by one of the bishop's staff, clergy have no choice as to who appraises them. In other schemes, where appraisal is voluntary, consultants may be chosen from lists supplied by the diocese. In one instance contracts are suggested for two years, then to be reviewed. In another instance it is suggested that no consultant should see more than five people, while in a more heavily populated diocese rural deans may have the assistance of a second consultant to deal with the number of appraisals that need to be conducted.

An appraisal interview, if it is to go into any depth, takes much longer than many schemes would appear to permit (see 'How often?' below), although three hours is recorded as being necessary in the recommendations of more than one diocese. In many schemes the interview is completely confidential, with instructions in one instance that no records are to be kept and permission asked even to make 'jottings' to act as an aide-mémoire in the interview. However, most schemes about which I have information make provision for the interview to be followed up in some way in writing. This may be through a summary which is recorded by both parties as a personal but private record; or it may be a summary written up by the consultant and signed by the person being appraised. One example suggests that such a report, although kept on file centrally, is held only until the next occasion of meeting, after which it is destroyed. Another requires a summary of the appraisal interview to be sent by the appraiser to the bishop, but insists that the actual appraisal form, completed prior to the interview by the minister, should be completely confidential, and the property of the appraisee.

Where schemes are more formal and compulsory and part of line management, reports are likely to be made to the bishop's staff. Only in one instance (now no longer in operation) do I have evidence of some information of a rather impressionistic kind being shared with the staff but not directly with the interviewee, although even in that instance the report was not retained after the staff meeting. In most instances it appears that any report has to be mutually agreed and that the appraised must have the opportunity to see what is written down, and where necessary make appropriate input for himself or herself. Only in this way can fairness and accuracy be ensured. Where schemes include the holding of appraisal information on file centrally, it seems generally as if there is a desire to safeguard the interests of the appraised.

Such concerns are unnecessary where schemes are both voluntary and not part of line management. While the essential confidentiality of appraisal is stressed, suggestions are also made for the sharing of information with diocesan officers, should the appraised person wish it. In one scheme the appraised person may ask the consultant to raise matters on their behalf with the bishop regarding the possibility of further training. In another, where ministers see training needs they are invited to communicate them to the Director of Education and Training. In a post-ordination scheme the bishop and all main parties are sent full reports, but the training officer is only sent the relevant sections.

I have little information concerning other means of follow up. Schemes seldom get as far as considering this when they are first set up. In the Liverpool JWC follow up is suggested, possibly through a phone call to see how things are progressing. I have only come across one example of a reaction sheet to the appraisal process, to be completed by the interviewee, indicating whether the exercise was found to be helpful or intrusive, with room for comments and suggestions for improvements. This was part of a pilot scheme. In Chapter 6 I suggest a form which might be of value to the consultants, especially in the initial stages of a scheme, to give them feedback from those they have seen and a means of comparing and contrasting the way in which both parties have perceived the value of the consultant's contributions.

Reference to the consultants themselves provides a further opportunity to look at the procedures used in the setting up of appraisal schemes. Training of consultants is fairly general, sometimes of a bishop's staff, often of teams of consultants. The requirement for consultants to be appraised themselves has already been referred to. Their training in some places may be a single training day on how to prepare for the interview, the skills required for the conduct of it, the structure and scope of the interview, defining key areas of ministry, and negotiating the monitoring of the process. Elsewhere it may be two training days, followed by quarterly meetings for support and further training, or a three-part course in interviewing run by a professional management training organization. In pilot schemes provision is normally made for a review session to be held after a year of project. Some schemes supply notes for the interviewers.

How often?

With so much local variation in design, approach and objectives, we might expect there to be similar differences in the frequency with which it is recommended appraisal takes place. In researching their report Hiscox et al. found 17 dioceses where there is annual appraisal. In other dioceses patterns vary, from one where new incumbents are seen after one year then every third year, to at least two others where there are three or four major interviews each year. Some dioceses adopt a pattern whereby the bishop sees each person once every three years but in between times they either see their own consultants or another member of the bishop's staff. As indicated earlier, the Liverpool Anglican Diocese has appraisal every three years but Joint Work Consultation as a separate, more confidential activity annually. Where appraisal takes place in the years immediately following ordination it is generally more frequent.

Ian Hardaker, to whose important paper I have already referred, suggests every two years for work appraisal, on the grounds that more frequent appraisal 'can lead to unhealthy introspection', and is difficult for diocesan staffs to arrange. He thinks that it requires between two and four hours to reflect on the questions which he suggests. While I believe he is right to allow a considerable amount of time for the interview, in my own experience of both appraisal and of pastoral counselling, it not only requires more time but also greater frequency if issues are to be addressed properly and followed through. Twice-yearly meetings are, to my mind, the necessary minimum to make effective use of an appraisal procedure; this frequency indicates not only the impossibility of a small number of consultants (bishop's staff or others) covering the ground, but also the need to make provision in any compulsory annual (or biennial or triennial) hierarchical scheme for additional consultancy arrangements for those who wish to conduct what I would regard as a healthy inspection of their working lives.

Overview

While it is impossible to sum up such a wealth of information about the appraisal schemes either in operation or under discussion as I write, the material furnished by papers (from mainly Anglican sources) indicates considerable thought and attention being paid to the subject. Not unnaturally the majority of documents circulating favour appraisal and point to its advantages. I have included many of these references in the section on the purpose of appraisal above and have mentioned such advantages in my opening chapter.

Clergy, like other people, clearly ask themselves how they are doing, and the schemes considered here aim to find someone who can help them answer their questions. Bishops certainly need information about their clergy, and some of the schemes help them to get this directly, while others provide avenues whereby information can be sent voluntarily to the bishop. Although appraisal runs the risk of being responded to, at least by some people, with suspicion, it is generally better that volunteered and checkable information should replace misinformation and hearsay. It is arguable whether appraisal meets the need of clergy for pastoral care, although it appears to provide grounds for hope that someone is interested in their work.

It is somewhat optimistic to think that the only new element about appraisal is that it is pastoral care undertaken in a structured and regular manner.[16] A more realistic description is perhaps, as the Liverpool JWC booklet suggests, that it 'bridges the gap between interference and indifference'.[17] There are, however, other considerations, touched upon in some of the questions I have raised in this chapter, which suggest the need for caution in the design and execution of appraisal schemes. These I will examine in Chapter 5, looking first at two schemes for ministerial and priestly development which merit particular attention.

Notes

1. From a private communication from Christopher Lewis, now Residentiary Canon, Canterbury Cathedral.
2. The fullest published description of appraisal in the Church in Britain appears in J. Mills and J. Nelson, eds, *Explorations into Parish Ministry: a guide to Joint Work Consultation*, Diocese of Liverpool 1983.
3. *Appraisal in Ministry*. Report of a Diocese of Liverpool Working Party, April 1987, p. 11.
4. *Report on Sector Ministries*. The National Society (Church of England) for the Promotion of Religious Education, 1983.
5. R. Hiscox, J. Gammell and C. Raybould, *Report of the Working Group on Appraisal and Assessment*. Prepared for the Church of England Continuing Ministerial Education Committee, May 1988.
6. Private paper circulated to diocesan bishops and others.
7. Some of the quotations in this chapter are from church youth organizations as well as diocesan reports or bishops' letters. These youth organizations include such church groups as the Boys Brigade, Catholic youth services, the Crusaders Union, other uniformed organizations, and groups from various denominations such as the Quakers and the Salvation Army, as well as information from the British Council of Churches and the Church of England Board of Education. The quotation appears in *Briefings 3*, November 1987, published by West Central Counselling and Community Research.
8. J. Mills and J. Nelson, *Explorations into Parish Ministry*, p. 18.
9. ibid., p. 21.
10. See, for example, E. Forshaw, *Mis-managing the Church*. Southwell and Oxford Papers on Contemporary Society, March 1988.
11. G. Barger et al., *The Institutional Chaplain — structures for accountability and assessment*. University of Nebraska at Omaha.
12. J. Mills and J. Nelson, *Explorations into Parish Ministry*, p. 22.
13. ibid., p. 23.
14. *Report on Sector Ministries*.
15. ibid., p. 52.
16. Ian Hardaker makes this observation in his private paper.
17. J. Mills and J. Nelson, *Explorations into Parish Ministry*, p. 5.

FOUR

Radical Reviews

Appraisal, as the previous chapter demonstrates, is currently developing in a variety of forms in response to the concerns of particular dioceses or sections of the Church, using locally designed initiatives or adaptations of other schemes. In this chapter I shall describe the work of two particular organizations which specialize in ministerial development. These do not refer specifically to appraisal, but it nonetheless appears to take place as part of a process of review and of ongoing personal growth. The programmes developed by the Centre for Human Development and by the Edward King Institute for Ministry have certain elements in common: both are essentially separate from the management of dioceses and independent of other forms of church organization; both use assessment tools (psychometric tests which are filled in at one stage, professionally scored at another); both incorporate a residential element; both concentrate on the whole person and not simply on the job; and both have their origins in the United States. They are, however, different and their programmes deserve separate treatment. Indeed, when checking the factual information in this chapter, one of the directors of the Edward King Institute told me that Ministry for Priests is more suitable for the Catholic system and their own for the Protestant system. The reader will need to judge, from the necessarily abbreviated description I give of their programmes, whether they are so obviously demarcated on denominational lines.

Ministry to Priests Programme

The Centre for Human Development in Britain, like its American parent body, serves Roman Catholic clergy through

its Ministry to Priests Programme (MPP).[1] This is 'designed
to stimulate priests to grow in every way, as priests, as
human beings, spiritually, intellectually, emotionally.'[2] Essential to its work is the conviction that each person is unique
and that no two journeys are the same; that growth is holistic
and that emotions and feelings, health, diet, weight, exercise,
are all integral parts of the spiritual life; that development
takes place through dialogue; and that the exercise which the
programme initiates is part of a lifelong process. Unlike the
programme of the Edward King Institute it is conducted
within a diocese, where the majority of priests have voted to
participate in it. The term 'majority' conceals the high degree
of support it normally has in practice (e.g. 80% in favour in a
typical diocese), although I qualify this large majority below.
Such 'ownership' of the programme by individuals and by a
diocese is an essential factor, since the initial stages require
the training of 'team members' selected from within the
diocese, who offer a peer ministry to priests. The programme
leads up to a report to the diocese as a whole. Following this,
the later stages are probably the most decisive factors as the
ongoing programme is essentially developed from within a
diocese, with the Centre acting as an external resource to the
diocesan Director of Continuing Education. At first glance
these developments look similar to Continuing Ministerial
Education in Anglican Dioceses, where diocesan appraisal
schemes have also been used as a means of identifying
training needs. The programme is, however, much more
extensive than anything in Anglican dioceses, bridging areas
which in many Anglican dioceses are covered by CME and by
Advisers in Pastoral Care and Counselling.

  Once the bishop and a majority of priests in a diocese
choose to participate in the programme through a vote of
commitment, a Director of Continuing Education and a team
of priests are nominated and appointed. It is this team which
will continue the programme. The team is larger than the
word implies, with about 10% of the priests in the diocese,
who are given intensive training in subjects like spirituality,
the ministerial role, and adult development, and in listening,
responding and assertion skills. This is in preparation for
their ministry to their brother priests which they take up

following phase one of the programme. (In fact 'sisters' would also be an appropriate inclusion, as religious communities may participate in a diocesan programme.) There follow one or more individual Convocation Days preparing the participating clergy for a five-day retreat, held on different dates to allow maximum participation. On the Convocation Day assessment instruments are offered to assist self-knowledge and to start the creation of each individual's personal, and confidential portfolio. Not everyone chooses to complete all four inventories, but the results of these questionnaires are fed back to individuals during the retreat. These provide a short cut to serious conversation and self-disclosure with a trained interviewer from outside the diocese, one of a smaller specialist team assisting at the retreat. The results are also collated to provide a very full profile of the participant clergy of the diocese as a whole, and details of this are included in the report which is later presented to the diocese.

An important aspect in the early stages of the programme is a 'personal growth plan' in which the individual is invited to reflect on questions in the four key areas of life: prayer; the physical; the emotional; and a fourth area known as intellectual-service-ministerial. One or two priority needs are selected from each section and recorded on a 'personal growth agreement' as goals, together with initial reflections on means of achieving those goals, realistic scheduling of them and a date for evaluating progress towards them. Assistance in completing this agreement is given by one of the trained team members, and the plan may be shared with someone else for support in achieving it.

Also during the five-day retreat the basic principles of the spiritual life are reviewed, with strong emphasis on the need for self-knowledge as a starting point. The programme makes use of Scripture and other spiritual writings, as well as of instruments developed by the behavioural sciences. At the end of the retreat each priest may choose a brother priest in the diocese (one of the larger trained team) with whom to go on working as a mentor and soul friend. The training which these team members receive is not sufficient for the Centre to want to call them counsellors—it is essentially a ministry offered by peers.

Peer ministry is one plank in a threefold structure which needs to be developed in a diocese following the retreat, the others being support groups and a programme of continuing education, so that by all three means there can be continuing and deepening growth. In peer ministry priests meet in pairs three or four times a year to look at their life and work. There is roughly one team member for every three or four of the priests who take up the recommendation for designing, implementing and evaluating personal growth plans.

Support groups of between six and ten members can form around people or around interests. A team member is assigned to each group to help it to form and work out its first covenant (or contract) for meetings, and to be in regular communication with a contact person in the group. Normally such support groups meet monthly, each meeting including an overnight stay, for the development of fraternity, learning, and personal and spiritual growth. Since the groups are formed through free choice, they vary in structure and objectives. Study, skills training, recreation and exercise, as well as prayer and relaxation together, are all different activities used in such groups. After the first series of covenanted meetings is completed, the group meets to evaluate its work and renegotiate commitment. It is suggested that groups may use a professional resource person or a facilitator to assist them, the former for specific areas of need, the latter as a more constant figure attentive to the group process as well as its content. The experience of the Centre is that groups which employ resource people or facilitators have been far more successful than those who do not.

The Centre for Human Development also writes a comprehensive diocesan report, in which a group profile of the diocesan presbyterate is developed, and in which recommendations are made for phase two of the MPP. The group profile pulls no punches, although of course the anonymity of the individual respondents is preserved by its very nature as a *group* profile. The confidentiality of such reports makes it impossible to reproduce any of their findings here, although it is to be hoped that in time the Centre may draw upon their accumulated data and share their knowledge with a view to assisting ministerial formation generally. A comparative study of Catholic priests and, for example, religious or clergy of other denominations or lay women and men could be immensely valuable to those whose task it is to promote personal growth and development in the Church. The levels of ego development and realization of personal potential, moral thinking and spiritual belief and practice, as well as the major personal concerns of the participant priests, provide a fascinating picture of the 'average' priest, against which the individual can measure his own scores. The report suggests that there will be consolation for the many who score around or below the average in discovering that others share their concerns and show similar characteristics; those who score above average may also realize that they have strengths in some areas with which to support their fellow priests.

This very full report, which includes specific recommendations to the bishop, the Director of Continuing Education, and the priests generally, is made available to all priests in a diocese. It is also a tool to be used by the bishop and the Director of Continuing Education in meeting identified needs. The responsibility for continuing the programme rests with the bishop, the ministry team and with individual priests. The Centre does not withdraw support and assistance, but its role changes from active leadership to supportive guidance. The Centre outlines the ways it can provide assistance for phase two developments, such as supporting the Director of Continuing Education, and meeting local leaders a year after the presentation of the report to evaluate its implementation. The Centre's initial two-year contract with a diocese is therefore only the beginning of years of potentially intensive work as the programme becomes rooted in the diocese itself.

Priests are appointed to the team of diocesan helpers on the basis of trust expressed in them by their fellow clergy. Although they are used by their brother priests in the development and implementation of a personal growth plan contract, material from these discussions is never used in appointment interviews. These helpers have their own team meetings, where they discuss particular problems in confidence but where no names are mentioned. Issues related to ministry can be raised through this forum and brought to the bishop for attention. All the bishops in a diocese are encouraged to take part in the programme, although for clergy generally participation in the programme is voluntary. Although approval in different dioceses has ranged from 66% to 91% of clergy voting, rather fewer follow the programme through to the retreat and personal growth plan, where take-up is around 50%.

In attempting to evaluate the success, significance and possible shortcomings of MPP, we are assisted by the American Center's own externally validated study of priests who have undergone the programme in the United States.[3] The fact that such a thorough evaluation has been made at all is one indication of the seriousness with which these linked Centres approach their work of ministerial development. 40% of the responses said that MPP had had a great effect in ministry; similarly 40% of responses said that it had had a great effect on relationships and on acceptance of life as a pilgrimage; 30% commented on the great effect it had had on physical wellbeing and 20% on the great effect it had had on the life of prayer.

The programme was frequently mentioned in written comments as a process of growth, sometimes even as a turning point. Respondents credited it with enabling them to make changes in their style of ministry and many also noted that it had resulted in a sense of common bond in their ministry. Detailed analysis showed that it was the structured follow up to the initial programme—support groups, one-to-one ministry, continuing education and team membership—which accounted for the reported effectiveness of the programme. The retreat and the psychological tools to assist self-knowledge, although they were remembered as especially valuable, do not in themselves seem to have been sufficient to enable change to take place.

In written comments support groups were mentioned most often as the main source of benefit of the programme; it appears that these groups also enabled certain changes to take place which other aspects of the programme did not, such as the ability to take time off without feeling guilty. The MPP had its strongest effect on what is called the 'emotional-relational' areas of the participants' lives, and the degree of impact was in direct proportion to the length of the individual's involvement in the programme's activities.

The study concerns the effectiveness of MPP and does not dwell on aspects of it which might be ineffective. It is, however, interesting to note that the three *lowest* categories for effectiveness of change in terms of average scores are, in descending order, study life, consistency in prayer, and relationships with the bishop. Although other evidence in the evaluation suggests that membership of a support group assisted changes in prayer life, and that membership of the diocesan team of peer helpers enabled priests to develop a closer relationship with the bishop, it is important to recognize that there may be some difficulties in ministry (amongst which study, prayer and relationships with bishops are not uncommon) which even the most thorough programme of personal development or appraisal will not easily resolve.

The evaluation paper's comment on the relative lack of importance of the psychological tests in effecting change confirms the limitations of mechanisms for 'rating'; examination of appraisal in commerce and industry has also shown these to be somewhat questionable. Impressive though the tests appear, there are some doubts to be raised about these 'tools of measurement', even when they are used (as they appear to be in the context of both MPP and the Edward King Institute) primarily to promote self-reflection. Psychometric, or personality, 'tests' and inventories are fast becoming popular in different areas of ministerial development, from training in human relations to spirituality, and those who have undertaken them appear to place considerable emphasis on their findings. All such tests, as the MPP reports point out, are prone to a certain degree of distortion by the person completing them. The tests depend on an honest and objective self-assessment, which is not always possible when, for example, high ideals lead us to see ourselves as we would like to be and not as we actually are. The MPP battery of tests, which together yield some interesting results in terms of the group profile, appear to show some discrepancies which call for further explanation. Compare, for example, the results of one set of tests to measure moral reasoning with the results of other tests to measure inner-directedness and ego development. A greater percentage of priests score 'high' or 'very high' in moral reasoning, suggesting they are relatively free from mere conformity to moral rules. But tests measuring ego development indicate a much smaller capacity for autonomous judgement. The results of these tests appear to be contradictory.

If there are some discrepancies arising from the group profile, what of individual profiles? Whereas the majority will feel some comforting sense of identity with their fellow priests, the results from a number of tests show some priests (albeit a minority) as having a high degree of conformity, a low view of human nature and considerable difficulty in perceiving themselves as persons of worth. We might be concerned as to how people with very low scores on any of the different scales cope with such results when they are pointed out to them. In fact very low scorers rarely reject the findings, nor do they go into a depression about them. Two points are made to them: firstly that a low score does not necessarily mean that they are not doing well; it can equally mean that their doing well is costing them a lot in terms of coping. Secondly it is important to see the tests not as objective but as specifically subjective: in other words it is not 'how you are' but 'how you see yourself' and self-perception (as I observed above) may be faulty, so that one person errs on the side of low self-esteem just as much as another might veer towards self-inflation. Indeed the analysis of the group profile expresses some scepticism about very high scores where they appear in any of the tests.

There is widespread acceptance of the value of the tests by those who participate in them. Sometimes the subjects say that they already knew about the findings, but even these people frequently add that seeing them set out in such a systematic way helps them to identify areas upon which they can work. We do need to remember, however, that these tests are scored and then discussed with the subjects by trained interviewers, and that their object is self-reflection and further discussion. Less careful, indiscriminate use of tests might otherwise lead on the one hand to narcissistic pride or on the other to hurt and pain.

In reading detailed reports of the programme (although without the advantage of having participated in one) I have been impressed by the way in which the MPP grasps the nettle of personal development and sees this as inseparable from the work of a priest. The psychological tests are an indication of the intimate involvement of the programme with the personality of the priest, as well as with his whole life style. It is fully recognized that this totality of the person, body, mind and spirit, makes an essential contribution to the quality of priesthood and that if people are to minister to others they will do this better when they embody the gospel message of reconciliation and freedom.

> Mediating the Good News through personal presence and dialogue demands an integration of reflection upon one's self and one's interior state; to accept one's self with both strengths and weaknesses and to trust in the basic goodness of one's body and emotions. It is necessary to allow others to be themselves, to transcend the images and stereotypes that ordinarily interfere with genuine encounter; to practice existential humour which manifests itself only at the higher stages of development.[4]

Furthermore the MPP puts strong emphasis on the collegiality of the priesthood, attempting to break the isolation which clergy so often impose upon themselves for one reason or another. The Director of the Centre in Britain accepts the criticism that the programme is too clerical and that a priest also needs to relate to the community in which he serves; but he also points out that for the moment it is clear that high on the list of concerns of Catholic priests is their need to relate more closely to each other, to rebuild a sense of fraternity and trust in each other and have someone minister to them rather than always minister to others. This part of the programme is very impressive, with support groups appearing to function rather better than they do in other denominations.

The programme also provides a good example not only of the appraisal (or more strictly the self-appraisal) of individuals, but also of review of the diocese itself in relation to ministerial development. The means exist whereby concerns expressed by individual priests can be passed on (anonymously) to those with authority in a diocese. Further examples of good practice are provided by the strong emphasis on training the diocesan team who will be responsible for furthering the programme, and the use of trained, external leaders of the first part of the programme.

Perhaps the very personal nature of the programme makes it essential that those who participate do so by choice and not under orders from their Ordinary. The philosophy under-pinning MPP, part of which includes the promotion of more personal autonomy and decision-making, clearly makes voluntary participation logical and desirable. Some dioceses have chosen not to engage in the programme. In those that have, as has been pointed out, fewer priests actually participate in the full programme than originally voted for it. However, opportunities exist for those who hold back the first time round or who come into a diocese later, to undertake the phase one programme (Convocation Day, tools of assessment, retreat and report). One Scottish diocese, for example, has had retreats every year for several years. Directors meet with their teams ideally once a month and the question is regularly addressed of reaching out to new priests and to those who are self-isolating. Once or twice a year the Centre arranges a retreat for interested people from across the country, and for new team members recruited to existing diocesan teams. The Centre also maintains regular contact with local directors with at least twice-yearly meetings, together with a three-day annual general meeting for training, sharing and celebration. All these measures help to maintain the impetus for ministerial development and support in a diocese, although much depends, of course, upon local initiative, drive and imagination.

Development in Ministry

The Edward King Institute for Ministry, administered from Lincoln, is mainly an Anglican foundation, although it is ecumenical in intention.[5] Its aims are as follows:

To promote and provide a service to meet the needs for professional development among men and women in ordained or duly authorised ministry in Christian Churches of all denominations . . . to encourage and publicise the study of issues affecting Ministry; . . . to co-operate with and participate in any programmes, projects and publications which will help the development and work of the Ministry within Christian congregations.

The Institute arranges a number of consultations for clergy which are held each year in a variety of locations throughout the country. It also provides a network for those engaged in the study of various aspects of contemporary practice in ministry. It is the consultation to which I give particular attention.

The Institute uses worksheets and ideas developed by Thomas E. Brown of the Center for Professional Development in Ministry, Lancaster, Pennsylvania. Four weeks before the consultation the participants are sent a workbook, which they begin to use at that stage. About six hours' work is required to complete four questionnaires, which remain the participant's property and are only shared at the consultation with the participant's permission. The initial work consists of a fourfold analysis: 1. of roles in ministry; 2. of abilities and skills, and what gives meaning to the person; 3. of the kind and depth of knowledge that they already possess; 4. a self-analysis, together with a personality test which is scored later and compared with the self-description.

This may seem like a lot of paperwork, and staff members are only too aware of the dangers of producing numerous pieces of paper and thereby failing to concentrate on the person. The initial questionnaires provide a springboard for four types of discussion and consultation at the four-day event, in which ideally there are nine participants and two staff members. The object of the consultation is to produce intentions for the future, so that looking ahead from the present is more important than looking back into the past.

Participants bring their workbooks with them and refer to them as they tackle singly, in threes and as a small group the four areas of analysis already outlined. They discuss, for example, their roles and those areas which they find satisfying, as well those where they feel less confident. The staff members try to help the participants to see that they have themselves identified their roles and that their roles are chosen, not simply thrust upon them by others. Using drawing as well as discussion, participants reach a point when they try to identify both who they are now and how they want to be, in relation to their work and in relation to God.

After a thorough analysis of these topics, the consultation moves into a new process, namely how to help participants reach the position of 'how they want to be'. They are given opportunities to identify the knowledge required and the abilities needed, as well as the characteristics desirable for the roles they wish to assume, and they compare these with their own self-analysis. What do they need to know, how do they need to be, what abilities do they need to acquire? The emphasis, as in the better types of appraisal so far examined, is on realistic objectives. The peer group of participants helps each member to clarify their objectives, sometimes challenging them from the experience they have built up about each other over their time together. What emerges is a list of what each person would like to develop in terms of knowledge, personality and skills. From the lists that are produced each person chooses three priorities for development, which again the group may wish to clarify or challenge.

The final session of the consultation consists of a period of 'brainstorming', during which members of the group are able to share their own ideas for resources and information with each of the group members. It is up to each individual to choose from this brainstorming what advice, if any, is useful and which suggestions they will act upon. Each person plans three clear objectives for action, and others in the group often pledge some assistance in supporting these intentions. As an example of what may happen in this last session, one member may have decided that she needs to increase her knowledge in a given area; she is provided with some ideas for reading by the rest of the group and she then decides to buy and read a particular book. Another member may offer to correspond with her to see how she gets on with the reading.

The Institute's consultations are especially useful if a person is at a major crossroads in ministerial development and wondering what decision to make, but they are equally valuable for those who feel stuck or bored in their ministry. Like phase one of the Ministry for Priests Programme, this is a once-for-all exercise, which hopefully leads to regular and permanent means for growth, development and support. It would be unusual to attend a second consultation, although at the time of writing the Institute has not been holding the consultations long enough to know whether it might be repeated ten or more years further on into ministry. The Institute has plans for a follow up on the formation of ministry, with the emphasis being on the integration of life, thinking and faith. This is intended as a deeper exploration, since the consultation on ministry is, in the modest words of one of its directors, 'rather like the *Readers Digest*'. My own impression is that this is understanding a process which provides an opportunity for a deeper exploration of role and vocation than is possible in an annual appraisal.

The initial worksheets sent out before the consultation act as a means of sifting out those for whom it is not the most appropriate step. The consultation is not suitable for those who are involved in a personal crisis. Selecting out those for whom this process would not be helpful also means that none of the consultations has given rise to personal crises in those attending. Participants are encouraged to take their own decisions and follow them through themselves, even though members of the same consultation may keep in touch with one another and provide each other with mutual support. Appraisal procedures and counselling are not infrequently two of the lines of action which participants choose to pursue.

The Institute respects the autonomy of those who have participated in the consultations and does not follow them up except in its own evaluation of its work. (The result of this evaluation was a very encouraging response and determination to press ahead with developing the workshops.) Participants are helped to decide their own priorities for ministry, their aptitudes and weaknesses, and their own goals for the future. Their work together is completely confidential and no report is sent to the home diocese. One participant to whom I spoke told me how much he had appreciated the experience and that he had come away from the consultation with clear objectives to follow through. He felt, as one of the directors also told me, that a person had to feel relatively 'OK' about their ministry to attend, and he was concerned that anyone who went in a state of depression about their ministry might dominate the rest of the group. Against this, I gather that staff members do not encourage the counselling style of relating amongst members of a consultation. This participant also felt that it was valuable to have had some consultancy or spiritual direction already and to have some ideas about the development of one's ministry before going, although my own conversation with the directors suggested to me that these may not be necessary for everyone attending. Although the consultations are not so closely tied to spirituality as the Ministry to Priests programme, regular worship is part of the four days together; and, as described above, the Formation of Ministry programme which the Edward King Institute is developing aims to integrate life, work and faith, making it holistic in its approach, as the Centre for Human Development also tries to be.

The two approaches described here are clearly different from annual appraisal, inasmuch as they tend to be one-off experiences which contain the possibility of enabling clergy to build regular support systems (such as appraisal) into their ministry. Nevertheless, the content of both programmes overlaps with appraisal, with the residential element providing both time and space, as well as psychological distance from work itself, for an extensive major overview of the state and direction of ministry. Perhaps it is the voluntary participation in the programmes, together with specially trained staff, and the uniqueness of the experience that enables both to look as much at the person as the work itself. The readiness to include the whole person in ministry is welcome, and may even be a feature of appraisal itself which needs to be considered in future developments.

Notes

1. The Director, Gerard Burke sj, is based at 23 Kensington Square, London W8 5HN.
2. Explanatory pamphlet issued by the Centre.
3. *Ministry to Priests: a study of effectiveness.* Washington DC, The Center for Human Development, 1983.
4. Private communication from the Centre.
5. The Edward King Institute for Ministry Development: Hon. Secretary: Norman Rudge, 51a Wragby Road, Bardney, Lincoln LN3 5XR. Honorary Directors: the Ven. Christopher Laurence and the Revd Canon Dr Norman Todd. The Institute also has links with the Alban Institute, Washington DC, the publications of which are available to EKI members at concessionary rates.

FIVE

Acknowledging Anxieties

The description of appraisal in preceding chapters, whether in the Church or in other contexts, raises various questions which need to be addressed, especially if appraisal is not to be adopted in a wholesale manner simply because it looks like the latest fashion in management tools. Since most appraisal schemes in use in the churches have been adapted from business or Civil Service models, we need to question whether such schemes can in fact be divorced from the setting in which they were first used, where there are clear lines of management and definite structures and limits to the work setting, and where most employees have agreed job specifications.

Clergy and other ministers in the Church have some justification if they claim that their work is different. It is in many cases a ministry which arises from the interaction of the personality and convictions of the individual and the unique circumstances of the setting in which it takes place, both the local church (with its own individual history) and the 'community' in which it is placed. It is easy to understand complaints that measuring productivity is, if not impossible, somewhat irrelevant (except in terms of statistics which provide limited information). It may be difficult to contemplate writing a job description which is clear and concise enough to be of any real value. The independence of the clergy is often highly prized; and indeed, where a minister does a reasonable job, we might expect him or her to perceive little in the way of management from above, except perhaps in respect of the wider Church. While those who occupy more senior positions in the Church are concerned with the management of resources (both personal and material), they are not normally expected to make much direct managerial

93

contact with the clergy, save perhaps for the purpose of appointments or occasional troubleshooting. Indeed, if we take Anglican clergy as an example, many (certainly amongst those who have been ordained for some years) would not expect, or even perhaps want, to see *too* much of their bishop, except for confirmations and other high points in the life of the local church when he may be a welcome guest — but essentially a guest and not 'the man in charge'! And there are many bishops who would not want to be seen as having to sanction initiatives of their clergy, as long as their ideas and actions are congruent with the teaching and mission of the Church. But we might also wonder whether some of the clergy who defend most strongly their independence of higher management (other than the conveniently distant divine higher management!) are of the kind who would find the idea of their own systematic management of the resources around them (people, plant and money) alien to the milieu in which they have been brought up, where ordination equipped them for almost anything, without the necessity for particular skills.

I may exaggerate to make a point but it is right to question how much validity there is in equating the way in which the Church and a commercial business are run. Some of the reservations about this have already been expressed in Chapter 2, where non-profit organizations were distinguished from business and industry. There are some important questions to ask which may highlight considerations promoting or preventing the design of an appraisal scheme that is at once effective for the minister and for the church in which he or she serves. If I pose these in antithetical form, I do not suggest they are exclusive; rather they are convenient forms for exploring the issues.

Minister or congregation?

Concentrating appraisal on the work of the minister runs the risk of neglecting the context in which his or her ministry takes place. The congregation, the environment in which the local church is situated, the relationship between churches, and the church and other bodies, the particular history into which a new minister comes—all these are bound to influence his or her work and in different ways to make it rewarding or frustrating. There are some settings which would test the patience of a saint! In individual appraisal the focus of interest upon the minister runs the risk of neglecting the background against which his or her work has to be understood.

There is another danger. It has been argued that it is particularly unwise to introduce appraisal for Roman Catholic priests when that particular Church is trying to promote collaborative ministry.[1] Appraisal, using as it does a professional approach to evaluation, raises the profile of the clergy as professionals and therefore as 'men apart' (the reference is to Roman Catholic priests). This concept is already too firmly lodged in the minds of the laity and needs to be dispelled if shared ministry of laity and clergy is to be encouraged on a more equal level. This argument has as much validity for other Churches: concentration on the minister leads to the danger of a retrograde step in respect of the ministry of the laity, the ministry of the whole Church. To appraise only the minister is to assume that the mission of the Church rests solely upon his or her shoulders. Furthermore, unlike the manager in industry, the minister cannot choose his or her 'fellow workers in Christ'; while he or she has a responsibility to nurture and develop the human resources within the parish and within the congregation, the clergy cannot 'appoint' the right people to the priesthood of all believers. He or she may be saddled with difficulties.

In an article whose title describes evaluation of clergy as a 'minefield', an American author, Roy Oswald, points out the dangers of appraisal when the relationship between pastor and people is strained.[2] The situation he describes is one where the local church employs the pastor and pays the salary; he or she is therefore much more accountable to the local church than is the case in episcopal churches in Britain, although some other denominations of course have the same system of the local church appointing (and paying) their minister.

I am not sure that the power of local appointment and payment is essential to Oswald's point, although it adds a particularly realistic dimension when he who pays the piper

calls the tune. Even if the clergy are more independent
(appointed from outside the parish, albeit after consultation)
trouble begins to surface between pastor and people if
evaluation of the clergy (as he calls it) is seen as part of the
solution to problems in a parish. Against this he warns that
'the truth of the matter is that we should only engage in
evaluation when things are going well, and studiously avoid
evaluation when things are going poorly'. When there is
tension between pastor and people, an entirely different
process of conflict resolution and problem solving is needed.

The same point can also be made even if there is no
particular trouble with or within the congregation: if a
person's ministry is going badly, then it is both dishonest and
also manipulative to use appraisal as a way of trying to get
problems out into the open, and or as a way of attempting to
change things. The problem has to be tackled directly, rather
than through the hope that appraisal will provide an answer.
Even open confrontation has to be done in the knowledge
that 'destructive criticism must be avoided at all costs.'[3]

Oswald suggests that it is valuable to link a parish audit
with clergy appraisal, so that the whole picture is looked at
and no one party can hand over responsibility to the other.
Otherwise clergy appraisal (and again here he is writing
specifically of evaluation by the employing parish) becomes a
way of scapegoating the clergy and a vehicle for expressing
negative feelings. This can also happen, we should note, in
clergy appraisal by someone outside the parish — the type of
appraisal which is most common in British churches. Instead
of appraisal of the clergy by parishioners becoming an excuse
to offload the parishioners' cumulative negative feelings,
appraisal of clergy by outside consultants may become the
focus for clergy grievances about the organization and/or the
institution of the Church. If this is given too much emphasis
clergy may omit looking at what and how they themselves
can change in favour of complaining about areas over which
they have much less control.

Oswald would prefer to see what he calls 'ministry
evaluation', in which the ministry of the whole parish is
appraised and not just the ministry of its full time professionals. It is for this reason that it might be useful to

consider a parish profile as part of appraisal, so that a minister looks at the setting of her or his work as well as the particular ministry exercised within it. This will be found in the suggested form for preparation for appraisal in Chapter 7. I also look at possible styles of parish audit, together with a wider remit for appraisal and review, in Chapter 9. Oswald is not completely dismissive of appraisal, but he makes a clear distinction between the evaluation of clergy by the employing parish (which he obviously holds to be dangerous) and evaluation in which the clergy themselves take the initiative; here they control the process, set the agenda and choose their own person to assist them from outside the parish — a much more common model in Britain.

While such warnings must clearly be heeded, there is another side to the involvement of parishioners or church officers which is potentially far more positive. They can be asked to help in the preparation for clergy appraisal; a minister can ask for feedback on different aspects of his or her ministry and invite one or two individuals in the local church to help him or her look at some of the appraisal questions. This preparatory involvement is quite different from asking for appraisal by the church members themselves; they are asked to act as assistants. I have some anecdotal evidence that where church members know that their minister is seeking appraisal from someone outside the parish, this encourages some of them to ask themselves questions as to how they might better support their minister. In one parish where problems from a previous incumbent had put great strain on the present minister, the lay officers began to address some of the issues only after he had told them he was going to undertake a review of his ministry. When this happens it clearly furthers the shared ministry of ordained and lay members of the Church and gives rise to joint responsibility and mutual support. Appraisal cannot take place in a vacuum, but has to be seen within the context of the local church; appropriately included in the process the local church will thus be helped to clarify its own aims and goals.

Voluntary or compulsory?

Both these terms convey the wrong impression about appraisal; the former may indicate a permissiveness which is liable to render any scheme toothless; the latter is redolent of a rigid or even repressive structure which is alien to the spirit of the older professions, where the professional is deemed to be able to act responsibly and independently, without the need for obvious coercion or instructions. Neither word is helpful and is best avoided in any reference to the subject. Compulsion may antagonize even those who would otherwise support appraisal, as an unnecessary interference with their cherished (if notional) independence. And a purely voluntary scheme is likely to miss the target. The clergy who could most benefit from appraisal are those most liable to avoid it if left to their own devices. We do not need to go as far as Oswald, who writes that the 'clergy who most need to hear evaluative data are least able psychologically to hear it', or that when things are going well no-one wants evaluation.[4] Some ministers may discover that appraisal helps them to identify priorities and supports them where they had feared it would be critical. But it may take a little leverage to get them to undertake it in the first place. Because resistance to appraisal has been anticipated, some schemes have deliberately been introduced with the emphasis on their voluntary nature; but those who most need it are amongst those who do not receive it, since they are not prepared to try it out.

Whether an appraisal scheme is introduced to make the organization of the Church more efficient (e.g. in providing better knowledge for appointments) or because it is believed to be of value to all ministers (whether they are more or less 'successful'), it is clearly better applied universally—a more positive way of putting it than 'compulsorily'. Unless appraisal is to be carried out by those who directly manage the clergy, a universal scheme need not interfere with the independence of the individual minister. Appraisal which stresses the benefits to the individual rather than to the organization, and therefore need not insist either on specific answers nor on divulging what has taken place, can be introduced as a requirement, with an approved list of consultants; only the fact that the appraisal has been carried out needs central notification. The content can remain private and the individual minister can choose what to discuss and what to keep hidden. In such appraisal it is the skill of the consultant, both in creating a trusting environment and in picking up areas of hidden concern, which determines the value of the process to the individual and which helps dispel the suspicions to which the introduction of appraisal might give rise.

Task-orientated or person-orientated?

There are obvious problems concerning the boundaries of appraisal, which we have already seen to be particularly difficult. Is it about the job, the person, or both? The Director of the Alban Institute Washington writes that because ministry is deeply personal this is one of the difficulties in conducting appraisal with clergy.[5] Other difficulties include the variety of tasks expected of clergy and the different tasks expected of those in different 'parties' in the Church.

It may be impossible, and indeed undesirable, to try to exclude the personal life of the minister, since the overlap is too great to make neat demarcation possible between person and parson. Well conducted, appraisal should in any case leave the initiative for raising issues with the person being appraised, so that while there is no unnecessary intrusion upon private areas of concern, personal matters can be raised. When schemes permit appraisal interviews to be confidential, such provision may encourage personal anxieties and perceived inadequacies to be shared.

Nevertheless, it is important to be clear about where the emphasis lies. Appraisal is more task-orientated than person-orientated; it is more about work development than about personal development; it is more about managing the job than managing personal emotions; it is more about public ministry than about personal spirituality. But having drawn out these contrasts it is already clear that neat distinctions are impossible. The way a person prays or understands spirituality will affect the way he or she conducts worship; the emotional stability or instability of the person will affect the way he or she manages and responds to people; personal development will make for better pastoral care, which is one of the tasks of the minister. So although consultants need to recognize where appraisal stops and where spiritual guidance or pastoral counselling begin (and even these two have hazy boundaries), the dividing line may be more in matters of technique than in matters of content. For example, a consultant only sees the minister once every six months or once a year. The technique for conducting a one-off session like that is quite different from a series of counselling sessions spread over a number of weeks, or ongoing spiritual guidance given perhaps every month. It is likely that the consultant will from time to time need to look into these other territories; but he or she has to judge how deep it is permissible to go, before commending other avenues of support and assistance. For example, a minister who has difficulty with boundaries between work and leisure may also have some difficulties arising from the need to be needed; and before he or she can begin to set firmer boundaries, attention may need to be drawn to some of the inner difficulties to do with self-acceptance. Similarly, recognizing the lack of clear boundaries between self and ministry means that a person may wish to talk about partner, family and domestic circumstances (particularly as in most cases the Church is responsible for the provision of private living space) as well as the job.

Although the evidence is again anecdotal, it has been suggested to me that clergy whose partner is supportive have a much more satisfactory and satisfying ministry than those whose partner undermines or denigrates their work; and that the close involvement which the clergy partner has with the job (by virtue of accommodation if nothing else) makes the role of partners more significant in ministry than in any other profession. It is not unknown, of course, in other professions for partners to be vetted as potential 'assets' for aspiring diplomats, politicians, and even top management. I do not wish to promote such a practice in the Church, nor to imply that clergy partners should not have a working life of their own. But if partners do have such bearing on the ministry of individual clergy, this suggests that some personal questions can be included on the agenda of appraisal and openings given for relationships to be discussed. I know of one bishop (and there may well be others) who always offers partners the chance to be present in appraisal, even though not all can or do avail themselves of this opportunity.

Simply because personal issues can be raised in appraisal we need to recognize how much more difficult this may make both the introduction and the experience of appraisal. It is important that the anxieties aroused should not outweigh the expected benefits of the exercise. Appraisal must not be seen as an unjustified invasion of individual privacy. Care must be taken that any information that comes from the sharing of a person's weaknesses and doubts is handled responsibly. Appraisal which opens up raw areas without applying any healing, is likely to be too painful an experience to bear repetition. And should strains, tensions and problems emerge which give rise to anxiety about a person's ministry, how does both the consultant and the Church cope with such revelation? An ACCM memorandum points out that 'while it may be true that a forgiven sinner is a better agent of God's good news than a righteous man, it is not a truth which is generally acceptable in practice.'[6]

Nevertheless, from the point of selection of candidates for the ordained ministry onwards, the Church looks at personal factors as well as depth of faith, academic ability and the right skills for the job. Personal development cannot be separated from work development, any more than it can from faith development.[7] And since such personal assessments are being made anyway in selection, training, making appointments and assigning responsibilities, it is perhaps more honest that they should be openly included in appraisal, so that, at the very least, the subject of other people's observations has space to reflect upon these matters for him- or herself.

Success or failure?

I have been conscious of wanting to avoid any notion of measuring success in ministry. This is partly because it is notoriously difficult to measure achievement in this and similar types of work. Pastoral ministry is not, for example, solely about administration. The role of clergy is much more difficult to assess than the functions of that role. What constitutes adequate performance? Numbers at services? Number of pastoral visits? Income raised? I commented in Chapter 2 about putting emphasis on the wrong things, because that way at least some measurement can be taken. The critical Roy Oswald (already quoted above) says that 'we seem determined to make evaluation a rational objective process.'[8]

There is, however, a second reason for being cautious about notions of success. As a former ACCM secretary has observed, popularity is not necessarily a measure of a good ministry, since the gospel sometimes requires a stand to be taken which is unpopular. After all, he wrote, crucifixion would be just as telling as a measure of good ministry.[9] While it is as undesirable to attach the specific appellation 'Christian' to appraisal as it is to a number of other areas of life, it may be necessary to develop particular standards and values for the assessment of ministry which are not always related to 'the ways of the world'. There is in the Gospels an apparent support for some aspects of the world, such as in the Parable of the Unjust Steward, or rendering to Caesar what is Caesar's, which would suggest that appraisal within the context of the Church need not be too different from appraisal in the secular world; but the gospel is also critical of society and some of society's ideas about success and reward, and it is this which adds another dimension to the underlying spirit in which appraisal might be conducted in Christian ministry.

Body of Christ or ecclesiastical organization?

This is, of course, an extreme way of expressing the alternative ways of understanding how appraisal, and various factors associated with it, fit with our image of the Church. In fact the two phrases need not be mutually exclusive, but for the present it is useful to identify two very different ways of understanding the type of corporate body the Church is and how authority, control and leadership are exercised.

On the one side there is strong belief in the Church as the Body of Christ with, if not infallibility, something close to it in the guidance of the Spirit. Within the limits set by the teachings of the Church, the exercise of ministry is almost independent of higher (human) authority. Clergy working on their own therefore tend to see themselves as primarily accountable to God and there is suspicion of anything which smacks of secular organization or technique. On their side such clergy can point to the way in which their independence has been encouraged in the past; they have been placed in parishes in the expectation that they will carry through their mission or priestly task without constant recourse to the centre. Not surprisingly they may stubbornly (as it seems to the new breed of managers) assert their freedom and freehold, and challenge the unnecessary invasion of the traditional view of accountability. Even bishops, who in their particular sacramental functions and as guardians of the truth are elevated to a high position, should not try to interfere with everyday parochial ministry.

Again I exaggerate. But if there is this side, there is also the other which urges the Church to see itself for what it is, an organization, and one which is as much in need of being organized and managed as any other; and since in most denominations the organization is also large and sometimes unwieldy there is an even greater need to order it efficiently. This view does not dispute that the Church is the Body of Christ but sees the problem less as a theological one than as a cultural one. In what he calls a 'rather tongue-in-cheek piece' Canon Forshaw writes:

> For better or worse the Church of England is a *man*-made institution and along with all other institutions stands and falls by the quality and effectiveness of its leadership. What it urgently needs is a new, radical style of leadership based on sound managerial principles.[10]

I spell out some of these principles below.

These two approaches to the question of organization and management must influence the way in which appraisal is designed, introduced, accepted and utilized. Into what type of management structure is it required to fit? There is little point, for example, in introducing appraisal as a requisite for every minister, with the results being communicated to the centre, if the centre does not know how to use that information effectively. It may not be right to introduce some aspects of management (of which appraisal is one) without going further to improve the management and the structure of the system it is designed to assist. Put another way, using the ideas of systems theory we also need to ask how the introduction of appraisal is likely to affect other aspects of the organization (see 'Central or peripheral?' below).

I am no authority on organization and management, but others can guide us in asking what type or types of organization the Church is. Etzioni describes three basic structures:[11]

a. *coercive*: such as those which contain prisoners and involuntary mental patients; members of these structures do not want to be there;

b. *utilitarian*: such as industry, where authority rests on power and reward, where members are motivated to earn and work in exchange for money;

c. *normative*: universities, medicine, the Churches, and other professions and voluntary groups, where the motivation comes from the nature of the work and where members are committed to organizational goals.

Such an analysis suggests that it would be unwise to introduce a particular form of appraisal from one structure without considering its effect on what may be a very different structure. It is better, for example, to foster commitment to appraisal as serving the organization's goals, than to be coercive.

A more complex typology, which is applied specifically to the Church, can be found in Rudge's study of ministry and management.[12] Each typology has a particular focus, method of organization, decision-making process, leadership style, and control process:

a. *the traditional*: here the focus is on maintaining a tradition regarded as of cardinal importance, where authority is vested in elders who guard the tradition. Control comes through loyalty to the tradition. Appraisal may be seen to be of value if it checks how faithfully the tradition is being adhered to and communicated to others;

b. *the charismatic*: here the organization focuses on enabling creativity and dynamism in the charismatic (or intuitive) person to flourish. Leadership tends to be prophetic and inspirational, and appraisal is perhaps very difficult, because it attempts to channel and order the creative force. Since both traditional and charismatic churches can be very critical of those other churches which do not share their basic tradition or assumptions, appraisal may be suspect, particularly if it comes from a different typology of the Church, such as:

c. *the classical*: where appraisal more naturally belongs, especially if it based on a design from commerce and industry, since the focus of the classical organization is on running the machine, efficient performance and accountability to lines above and below, and control is by 'specific standards set by top management';[13]

d. *the human relations model*: where groupwork and relationships are the primary focus; although this may seem my natural choice, this model of organization tends to be highly disorganized if left to itself, since it is essentially non-directive in its pure form. It is, however, believed that movement takes place better through consensus than through coercion. Although action often takes longer to effect, there is evidence to support the opinion that after time taken in talking and agreement action tends to be swifter and better motivated. Whereas authoritarian ways of control may mean swift decisions, there is often reluctance to put the decisions into effect if those required to take the action have not been involved in the decisions themselves and are therefore less well motivated. The appraisal model that is most acceptable here is one which in the first instance has been agreed with the participants, and which provides sufficient space for an open agenda, where the participant is encouraged to take the initiative.

e. *the systemic model*: here the system is seen as a living organism and focus of organization is on helping it to adapt to change. My own preference is for this model, which attempts to maximize relevance, stresses interdependence and adapts rapidly to change. Authority tends to be vested in experts and those who can monitor change and clarify goals. Appraisal within such a model focuses on enabling people to review what they are doing: relating effectiveness to broader perspectives than simply accountability to those above or below and looking particularly at monitoring ministry and setting goals. If the Church, in a world of rapid change, is to be adaptable to new circumstances and to constant review of its goals and of its methods of achieving those goals, then appraisal may be a very important part of ministry in this model. But this is a big 'if' which others, particularly those who prefer the traditional model, would disagree with, since they might maintain that the Church needs to represent the rock-like stability of traditional values in a too rapidly changing society.

Although my preference is for the systemic model, I recognize some potential value in each of the five types of organization. In the implementation of appraisal, it must constantly be borne in mind that these typologies are more than theories — they symbolize attitudes which are deeply held within different parties of the Church and by clergy of different traditions. While it may be difficult for one method of appraisal to be all things to all people, the systemic typology suggests that some adaptability of its content and conduct may be essential if it is to be more or less universally accepted and valued.

> Management and supervision are two words rarely heard here until recently. It has therefore been very difficult . . . to initiate clear lines of accountability, management and supervision. These are now beginning to emerge, but it is all rather strange within a Church structure such as ours.[14]

Rudge's analysis might make us question whether management or accountability is that strange, since each typology has its particular way of structuring leadership (or management) and its own version of accountability (as the charismatic's accountability includes 'testing the spirits to see if they are of God'). It is the introduction of other avenues of accountability that may be strange.

Forshaw, in the paper quoted above, stresses the need for accountability alongside the need to overhaul the management and government of the Church of England, and the need for a career development plan for its ministers.[15] Such organizational matters are by and large beyond the scope of this book, although the management structure and paths for career development have relevance to the introduction of appraisal. Is appraisal likely to be of much value if it takes place in isolation from other changes?

The dilemma can be seen in the problems which an Anglican diocese might have if a system of appraisal is instituted by its equivalent of 'line managers' — the archdeacons and suffragan bishops. It is impossible to develop a programme for appraisal which provides the ratio of one senior staff member to half a dozen clergy appraisals per year, which we have seen to be the requirement in Marks and Spencer.[16] Most schemes which are designed to be conducted by senior staff permit only one appraisal interview every three years. There is some use, in more than one Anglican diocese, of rural or area deans, who might be seen as similar to middle managers and to whom parish clergy go for appraisal. But the rural or area dean scarcely has the time or the resources to act efficiently in this intermediate level of management when he (and it is likely to be a 'he') has his own parochial ministry to manage as well. Forshaw calls them '"episcopal errand boys" rather than a key link in the chain of command.'[17]

Some dioceses have deliberately chosen consultants for appraisal outside the hierarchical structures; but others have had to institute (from necessity or choice?) a dual system; one interview every three years with a bishop and a voluntary system with choice from a panel of consultants for times in between. These factors will certainly influence the way in which appraisal is viewed and used in an organization, pushing it on the whole in the direction of supporting the individual minister rather than in the direction of serving the whole organization.

Career development may seem a strange notion to introduce in churches where there is, for the majority, little chance of moving beyond incumbent (or equivalent) status. Forshaw, as others have done, criticizes the method of appointment of senior men in the Anglican Church. He quotes one disbelieving managing director as asking: 'Have I got it right, neither of the two named men for this specific "top job" [a diocesan bishop] know beforehand that they are in line for this assignment; or are interviewed for the job when they have been "selected", or subjected to a personality aptitude or psychological test, or an assessment of their wife's (if they have one) willingness or capacity to be a bishop's consort . . .'[18] Nor are things necessarily much healthier at lower levels of appointments, where vacancies are infrequently advertised. Indeed it used to be thought in Anglican circles not thirty years ago that a parish needing to advertise for a priest must have something wrong with it.

Career development is not always about promotion; it also includes moving to new places in order to develop new insights and skills, or in order to carry specially developed aptitudes and ideas into a particular setting which might be able to make use of them. Career development can be of mutual benefit to the minister, the local church and the wider Church. Through appraisal ministers can be asked where they might like to be in five or ten years' time and what particular training or experience they need to help to get them where they would like to be. It enables unrealistic hopes and expectations to be faced, and achievable personal goals to be set.

There is another aspect to all that goes with the improvement of management and organizational structures, which has relevance for appraisal, the question of job descriptions which I look at below.

Job or vocation?

There is no reason why the vocation to the ordained ministry or the belief that ministers are called by God to serve in different places within the Church need conflict with the value of a job description, which more than anything lays down the lines of accountability and the main responsibilities of the office-holder. Non-stipendiary ministers in the Church of England are now required to have a job description, and one bishop writes that 'in the case of a second curacy or a lay worker or a non-stipendiary priest, an attempt should be made to write a job description before the appointment is agreed, so that on each side people are clear about what is expected. That can be reviewed and maybe rewritten each year.'[19]

It is important to notice that the job description is an agreed one, that it is negotiated from both or all sides, and furthermore that it can be rewritten each year. Perhaps, indeed, it should be reviewed as a matter of course after one year. Where there is an appraisal procedure this can take place regularly; and the appraisal procedure can itself make use of the outlined responsibilities as an agenda for reviewing the particular ministry. A job description is made for people, not people for the job description.

Obviously when making an appointment the job description has to be drawn up by those who are advertising the post and by those who are involved in working with the person required. A parish profile will also be a necessary requirement, including in it reference to any problems experienced under the previous 'management' of the minister who has recently left. Job descriptions may be revised in the light of an interview; but in any case they act as a preliminary statement of priorities, which must be reviewed in the light of experience. A job description for a County Council post, for example, clearly states: 'The main activities listed below may need to be revised in the light of experience. After an appropriate period in post, the duties and responsibilities can be clarified, and, if necessary, given a different emphasis.'

We should also note that job descriptions may or may not include the skills and knowledge required of the person to be appointed. Normally these are included in the particulars of the appointment and therefore also need to be thought through and described as precisely as possible. But it is valuable to separate them from the job description, since once a person is appointed it would be unusual to ask for a different set of skills and knowledge from those asked for originally;

appraisal may, however, include some time on the possibility of further education or training in order to develop skills.

A good example of the inclusion of the required skills, knowledge and aptitudes of applicants appears under the heading 'person specification' in a sample job description in the report on sector ministries.[20] It includes this outline of the abilities and qualities expected of a Social Responsibility Officer:

> Lay or ordained, must have theological competence, some knowledge of sociology of religion or related fields. Several years experience in social work or similar, experience of aspects of local government desirable, expertise in communication essential. Should be willing to work some weekends and some evenings, etc.

The following is a useful outline of the necessary headings in a job description:[21]

Job Title:

Area, church, diocese: this is kept very brief. A fuller description of the parish, for example, is a separate document.

Purpose of position: this often starts 'to improve . . . to create . . . to develop . . . to provide . . .' It is an overall statement of the aims of the job.

Tasks (or responsibilities): this lists the different elements of the job, normally in no more than 10 to 15 points. It may be broken down into sub-sections e.g. pastoral; administrative. Typical tasks might be promoting involvement in the Council of Churches or training and supporting leaders of house-groups. It might also be important to include some statements which make it clear that certain tasks are *not* the responsibility of the office-holder, e.g. he or she will not be responsible for fund-raising.

Skills: where these are included they are kept brief and are related to the task section.

Relationships (or those for whom the person is responsible): since ministry is so much to people, this will be an important section. It describes the groups and/or individuals the person needs to relate to, and the nature of the relationship: e.g. to support the youth organizations; to train and appraise junior staff; to work as part of a hospital chaplaincy team.

Accountability (or those to whom the person is responsible): an example of this might be a bi-monthly church council meeting or the archdeacon or suffragan bishop. If appraisal is to be included as part of the procedure of accountability, then this might be included here; however, confidential appraisal arrangements with an independent consultant are better included under 'responsibilities' than under 'accountability'.

Central or peripheral?

I have to overcome the temptation to see this final section as tidying up a number of loose ends concerning anxieties about appraisal. But to see these particular matters as loose ends is already to fall into the trap of making them appear less significant than they are. If appraisal is introduced as a central activity, an essential part of the annual round of ministry, then certain implications need to be faced and given priority. Otherwise appraisal may easily become an activity to which lip service is paid, with clergy simply going through the motions, but which is increasingly seen as an irrelevant, ineffective and interfering requirement by the employing church.

Simply stated, we need to recognize that appraisal procedures are time-consuming, that they need to be conducted well, that they require trained consultants or staff, and that the conclusions emerging from individual appraisals and general feedback may require more emphasis to be given to certain aspects of training, or to the need for urgent action and change in the employing church. Appraisal, in short, will cost money.

Consultants need training and support to sharpen their skills. They need their expenses covered. Regular feedback sessions are necessary not only to support them but also to enable general findings about ministry to be shared (without divulging the details of individual appraisals). Since, as I have constantly stressed, the ratio of appraised ministers to one consultant must not be too high (ten to one is mentioned as a reasonable figure in one report), there are questions about how such numbers of consultants are chosen, how they are trained and how their work is monitored. It is vital to recognize that the appraisal interview is as delicate and probably as difficult as an initial assessment interview for pastoral counselling—and that the skills to conduct useful 'one-off' sessions are greater than those needed for general pastoral care. There needs to be, for instance, a fairly rapid decision about the goals for any one meeting, so that time is not wasted and the agenda limited to what is possible; this requires a sharp mind and careful steering, while at the same time allowing the appraised person to set their agenda and to go at their own pace. There will be little chance, except after a fair interval of time, to follow up unanswered questions or remarks or feelings between appraiser and appraised that might have caused anxiety or hurt. The conduct of the appraisal session needs to be taken seriously, as an occasional meeting upon which much might depend.

I have suggested at several points that use might be made of generalized information coming from a series of appraisals, as well as the agreed shared information coming out of particular appraisals. An appraisal scheme will therefore need a mechanism whereby questions, information and requests can be shared with others. There is always the possibility that appraisal will open a Pandora's box; that either long-nursed grievances about the way the Church treats ministers or even more personal stresses may be aired and shared once given the opportunity. Unless there is follow up and potential for action, opening such sores may do more harm than good. So, churches will need to ask what resources they have available financially and in terms of skilled personnel, to handle whatever comes. Introduction of appraisal may, in more sense than the theological, be a somewhat eschatological event!

Notes

1. Bernard Kilroy of Trent Polytechnic argues this in an unpublished paper.
2. R. Oswald, 'Clergy Evaluation: a map of the minefield', *Action Information*, Washington DC, The Alban Institute, 1988.
3. *Report on Sector Ministries.* The National Society (Church of England) for the Promotion of Religious Education 1983, p. 51.
4. R. Oswald, 'Clergy Evaluation'.
5. L. Mead, *Evaluation: of, by, for and to the clergy.* Washington DC, The Alban Institute.
6. Advisory Council for the Churches' Ministry, 1980.
7. See M. Jacobs, *Towards the Fullness of Christ.* Darton, Longman and Todd 1988.
8. R. Oswald, 'Clergy Evaluation'.
9. R. Reiss, in a private paper.
10. E. Forshaw, *Mis-managing the Church?* Southwell and Oxford Papers on Contemporary Society 1988.
11. E. Etzioni, *A Comparative Analysis of Complex Organizations.* New York, The Free Press of Glencoe, 1961.
12. P. Rudge, *Ministry and Management.* Tavistock Publications 1968.
13. ibid., p. 33.
14. *Briefings 3.* West Central Counselling and Community Research, November 1987.
15. E. Forshaw, *Mis-managing the Church*, p. 6.
16. Marks and Spencer Training Department, *Appraisals.* Marks and Spencer plc 1987.
17. E. Forshaw, *Mis-managing the Church*, p. 5.
18. ibid., p. 1.
19. David Sheppard in J. Mills and J. Nelson (eds), *Explorations into Parish Ministry: a Guide to Joint Work Consultation.* Diocese of Liverpool 1983, p. 18.
20. *Report on Sector Ministries*, pp. 22–3.
21. W. Feek, *The Way we Work.* Leicester, National Youth Bureau, 1982. I have included in with his headings phrases from actual job descriptions in the caring professions and some suggestions made by Tim Herbert in the job descriptions included in his unpublished thesis *The Nature and Purpose of the Stipendiary Ministry in the Church of England.*

SIX

Insights into Interviewing

Looking at myself

Whether the emphasis in appraisal is on self-appraisal or on appraisal by a second person, undertaking such a task involves putting 'me' under the scrutiny of myself or of another. How I view such careful examination influences the way I approach appraisal and how much I respond to what I see or am shown in the process. If I approach appraisal with an awareness of being under some sort of judgement or criticism which I feel may put 'me' to shame, and hence make 'me' feel bad, I will be less sure of whether I want to look too hard in case I discover things which provoke severe self criticism; or I will exaggerate the importance of my successes; or I will tend to gloss over those aspects of my work about which I feel unclear. I will either be dismissive of comments made to me, or provide unnecessary excuses, or feel so bad inside myself that I wish I had never agreed to appraisal in the first place.

Although we talk about the self as if it were a unified concept, in self-appraisal one side of my self is looking at another side of my self; I become my own observer. But is the observer what psychologists have called the ego—a mature discriminating part of the self? Or is it what some call the superego—that particular type of conscience which includes a sadistic element that so often leads to feelings of shame or guilt? The ego, especially when it is strong and able to resist the worst excesses of the superego, is relatively free of the need to make value-laden judgements, although it still makes judgements of what is true or what is effective without getting into moralizing terms such as 'good' and 'bad'. The superego, on the other hand, tends to fasten upon rights and wrongs and to reward or punish on the strength of what it finds. Too strong a superego will turn my appraisal into a torture chamber.

Another way of framing the same internal process is to use terms from Transactional Analysis. When I appraise myself or am appraised by another, is it an adult-to-adult interaction, or do I make myself feel like a child under the critical gaze of a parent figure? Yet a further way of expressing the internal process in appraisal is that I set alongside each other my aims and ideals, and my actual performance. If I have set ideals for myself in my work which are achievable or nearly achievable, they act as an incentive to action and progress; but if I have erected for myself too lofty a set of ideals, and in addition make myself suffer when I fall short of them, they become perpetually pressurizing reminders of how far I am from my own over-ambitious objectives.

Yet appraisal would be meaningless if it did not involve a degree of judgement and criticism, to which I alluded more theologically in Chapter 1. In fact the sort of criticism which is required of ourselves or of our appraiser is like that in Biblical or literary criticism — a discerning eye, which is more concerned to analyse and understand than to tear apart and condemn. And the term judgement is like that used in a court of law — the interpretation and understanding of evidence, and arriving at an accurate verdict, rather than the punishment which is subsequently passed should a person be found guilty.

However, it would be idealistic of me to imagine that the majority of those who engage in appraisal or self-appraisal can fully practise that kind of objective and rational understanding just described. Even if it is true that appraisers are not judging us in a condemnatory sense, it is easy to feel, in some small corner of the breast, that twinge of anxiety that they are. Therefore it is essential to acknowledge that the process of appraisal is bound to give rise to personal responses, some positive and some negative, some strong and some innocuous, which will influence the way in which the task is approached and reacted to. It is necessary to assume, until there is evidence to the contrary, that the person being appraised *is* going to be sensitive to criticism. This will mean exercising care that remarks which are intended to be constructive are not expressed in ways which appear destructive. It means framing critical comments with an awareness of the difficulties a person may experience in receiving them. Despite the utmost sensitivity, there will always be some taking part in appraisal procedures who are liable to view even the most supportive remarks as suspicious, and to interpret pats on the back as likely to contain some venomous sting in the tail!

On the positive side, a well-conducted appraisal can have a healing effect, helping some of those who suffer from excessive self-criticism to discover, through the acceptance of their consultant, a more generous attitude to themselves. Their own ego can be strengthened by seeing the observer ego of the consultant at work, so that they too learn to be critical in a creative sense, and take less notice of that sadistically critical part of their reactions which in their daily work sabotages self-confidence and inhibits initiative. Much the same process happens in pastoral counselling, although in counselling the opportunities for this type of change in attitude to oneself are greater because the therapeutic relationship is more continuous.

Those who are more at ease with themselves (by which I do not mean people who are good at everything) will probably benefit from appraisal from the start. Their ego will be their observer, they will soon realize that their own self-appraisal is enhanced by the observations of a second person. Their appraisal is likely to lead to a fairly objective, encouraging and creatively critical view of the self and of their work. Where aspects of work have not gone well, these will not be equated with themselves as a whole; even if some areas of their work have gone badly or been unrewarding, this will not shake their basic sense of self-worth. They will be able to distinguish between those things which are their responsibility and those which are inherent in the situation.

But there will be others, however good their work may be, who will experience difficulties in appraisal because of the threat which is presented to their self-esteem. Their self-judgements, or their perceptions of the judgements of others, will invariably be on the harsh side, and their ideals will be unattainable and relentless. The combination described above of a sadistic conscience and impossible ideals will be such that attempts to appraise work or self will create an uncomfortable tension. As a result such ministers may refuse to participate or to take the exercise seriously; or, if their conscience tells them they ought to take part, they may end up in a state of demoralization. These will be people whose conversation tends to be peppered with 'oughts' and 'shoulds' and 'musts'.

The dynamics of learning

Although appraisal of ministers cannot avoid touching on these personal responses, nor avoid including within the appraisal of ministry some of the personal factors which contribute to and result from the effectiveness of that ministry, it is in fact a very different process from pastoral counselling. In pastoral counselling the client is encouraged to regress, to get in touch with those aspects of the personality which irritate and cause difficulties to self and others. Emotions are stimulated by the therapeutic situation, as well as by the outside problems which the client brings. It is a way of learning, and it requires the participation of the adult side of the client as much as appraisal does. But the basic needs of the person on the one hand, and the threatening rule-imposing demands of the person's superego on the other hand, are allowed to surface because they form the raw material of the counselling work.

Appraisal is a much more obviously adult-to-adult exercise. It too is a way of learning, but a way of learning which in this case can be impaired by child-like needs or self-imposed demands. As in all learning situations, participants need to enter what Hartung calls 'the latency mode'.[1] Taken from Freud's description of the age from approximately five to twelve years, the latency mode means a state of mind which is not dominated by over-strong feelings from earlier developmental stages—needs or demands which I have described elsewhere as including trust and dependency, authority and autonomy, and co-operation and competitiveness.[2]

The first requirement of the latency mode is that we are able to learn from someone who is competent; the second is

that we ourselves need to be 'relatively free of the continual
stimulation of oedipal and pre-oedipal themes in order for
energy to be available to put into the task of learning.'³
Hartung means by this that teachers (or consultants in
appraisal) are there to teach (or to consult) and not at that
time to fulfil other roles — they will not be able to teach or
appraise if I am more anxious that they should be a soft or a
seducing parent, an oracle of indisputable advice or a chatty
friend, rather than a person of wisdom (which includes
ignorance) and discernment.

If we are not relatively free of unresolved issues, particularly
in relation to parental and other authority figures, there will
be difficulties in learning from appraisal. We may not be able
to listen attentively to the appraiser because he or she is seen
as authoritarian or inhibiting. We may find it difficult to talk
about certain issues because of fear of experiencing mistrust,
shame or guilt — the three opposites of the positive qualities
of trust, autonomy and initiative which are laid down in the
early stages of personal development and which the relationship between appraiser and appraised needs to foster. The
appraiser may in some way be feared, hated or despised or,
the opposite, endowed with such an aura that the appraised
person puts him- or herself in the shade. Feelings of rivalry
may give rise to a competitive relationship with the appraiser,
in which the appraiser is seen as more successful and in some
way showing the appraised person up. Or, less obvious, but
by no means uncommon in those who put themselves down,
feelings of competition can lead to the inability to accept that
in some aspects the appraised person will have done a far
more successful piece of work than the appraiser has yet
achieved. There is no value in false modesty.

Hartung also makes the point that the teacher (or in this
instance the appraiser) needs to have mastered these same
'oedipal and pre-oedipal themes': unnecessary competitiveness, the need to exert authority or the wish to encourage
dependency in the appraiser will all prevent the appraised
person from growing in confidence, autonomy and independence. Indeed the best appraisers may be those who, having
learned from their own successes and mistakes, can help
those they appraise to discern more quickly the stronger and

the weaker points in their ministry, so that the ministry of the 'next generation' can build upon, and eventually surpass, the experience of the appraiser.

Two further considerations in the process of appraisal are suggested by a paper on supervision by Searles.[4] Appraisal is likely to be a requirement (even if it is 'voluntary' there will be moral pressure to participate), and requirements can easily be seen as constrictions on, rather than opportunities for, growth. The appraiser will need to be aware of the feeling in some ministers that appraisal is something that has to be done and to be got through as unmarked as possible. They attend because they have to rather than because it is something they believe in. As is the case when resistance is shown in the counselling setting, time is better spent initially upon the feelings a person has about appraisal itself, in an attempt to understand the resentment and anxiety, instead of pressing on through the agenda regardless.

The second consideration which Searles suggests the supervisor (and appraiser) should have in mind is that the person appraised may feel caught between the criticism (explicit or implicit) of patients (or in ministry people in the parish) on the one hand, and fear of the appraiser's disapproval on the other. He emphasizes how important it is to understand the difficulties which people may be experiencing which come less from themselves and more from those with whom they work; and the need then to support them in their self-esteem.

Defensive strategies

Foskett and Lyall, in a parallel book in this series,[5] have already made more available to the reader the description given by Kadushin[6] of the types of games which can be played in supervision. These games apply equally to appraisal, and for that reason bear repetition and some licence in adapting them to the context of appraisal. The term 'games' is unfortunate if it diminishes the seriousness of the threat which is felt, to a greater or less extent, by all who are being supervised or appraised. If the appraiser is made aware of some of the ploys which are used to avoid the task, and of the need to avoid collusion, he or she also needs to understand the feelings which might give rise to defensive strategies. No-one is simply being 'awkward'.

Like supervision, appraisal gives rise to anxieties; it implies that change may follow, and involves a critical examination of ideas and practice and, as we have seen to be almost inevitable, of some aspects of personality too. Any change which results from appraisal will involve giving up old patterns. It is worth repeating that the relationship with the appraiser means giving up cherished independence and autonomy in order to allow another to see one's work. It means sharing one's ignorance. There is always the fear, as seen above, of criticism, shame and even rejection. It is not surprising, in the face of all this, that there is likely to be a desire on the part of the person being appraised to keep losses to the minimum and to maximize the rewards from the encounter.

Adapting Kadushin's examples (as Foskett and Lyall have done for pastoral supervision) the following 'games' have some relevance to the interactions in appraisal:

Two against the Church, or seducing by subversion

Since appraisal is likely to involve a certain amount of form-filling in preparation for the interview, and since appraisal may be felt to be imposed from above, the minister may try to get the appraiser to hook into his or her own irritation with authority and bureaucracy: if the appraiser shares some of this frustration, either about the appraisal scheme or about his or her own relationship to the Church, the time can be eaten into with mutual complaints about fulfilling particular requirements. 'No wonder I can't get visiting done, what with all these things the diocese now requires of us.'

Be nice to me because I am nice to you

'I am glad I've got you as my consultant: I've always heard such good things about your ministry; I'm going to learn a lot from you.' Such remarks may be genuinely felt and yet may also have the effect of softening up the consultant enough to prevent him or her saying anything too penetrating about the minister for fear of tarnishing the idealized image which the minister has initially communicated.

Protect me or treat me, but don't beat me

Since ministry involves personal factors which cannot be totally ignored in appraisal, the minister may in this instance try to forestall feared criticism of the work by exposing her or his own difficulties instead of the ministry itself. In fact the appraiser cannot solve personal problems and should be aware of other resources where such difficulties can be taken if necessary. Personal problems may need some clarification for the appraiser to assess how much they have interfered with the exercise of ministry. But appraisal concentrates on better management of work issues, which may itself lessen stress and enhance confidence. Being asked to offer pastoral care and counselling may prove tempting to the consultant who is more familiar with that than with the role of appraiser.

Heading them off at the pass

Anticipating severe criticism, the minister in this variation on the above game concentrates upon her or his work setting and so freely admits all the mistakes that have been made and so acknowledges that things have not gone well, taking such responsibility for them, that the appraiser is hard pressed not to sink into sharing the gloom; he may then spend the time reassuring rather than examining what constructive changes might be considered.

Appraisal is not for friends

Alternatively, the minister may suggest a meeting which is designed to heighten informality, and remove the potential threat of working on the appraisal itself. This may involve inviting the appraiser out for lunch, thinking appraisal can be conducted in a social atmosphere, or wanting the relationship to be a friendship, where no work can be demanded or done.

Maximum feasible participation

Most forms of appraisal combine particular questions, asked in the preparatory literature, with space for the appraised minister to select the key areas of concern. Since this kind of involvement and participation of the minister in the agenda is encouraged, it may not be easy to spot those times when certain areas of ministry have been selected for attention but others kept at a safe distance. Thus the minister takes advantage of the offer of full participation in setting the agenda to talk about things that are going well, to the exclusion of things that are causing worry. It requires subtle perception to spot such resistance and sensitive support (e.g. of those things that *are* going well) before confronting it.

If you knew Dostoevsky like I know Dostoevsky

The delightful title of this game is expanded by Kadushin into the student social worker making 'a casual allusion to the fact that the client's behavior reminds him of that of Raskolnikov in *Crime and Punishment*, which is, after all, somewhat different in etiology from the pathology that plagued Prince Myshkin in *The Idiot . . .* you do remember, don't you?' In appraisal the equivalent may be the citing of technical information or specialist knowledge which may make the appraiser feel he is ignorant and the last person who should be guiding someone else in their ministry. Alternatively, the minister may engage over-intellectually in the task, generalizing about theology rather than looking at her or his specific work.

So what do you know about it?

Where those in senior management positions act as consultants for appraisal, one way of reducing the disparity between senior and junior position may be for the appraised person to gently disparage the credentials which the appraiser has for being able to offer anything valid: 'I don't suppose you remember what it was like . . . You've not had a lot of parochial experience yourself, have you? . . . It's different for a single man, but you married clergy wouldn't know that . . .' etc.

It's all so confusing

As an alternative to the above, the minister cites different authorities or directives, other appraisers or mentors, implying either that these have given a completely different analysis or advice, or that everyone says something so different that the minister is left bewildered. Either way may prevent the situation being looked at in detail.

I have a little list

The minister makes full use of the preparatory form for self-appraisal, and brings such a long list of items to talk about that each one can only be skimmed over briefly, and none can be looked at in any detail or depth. I suggest in the next chapter that each session of appraisal may usefully be limited to one specific area of ministry.

What you don't know won't hurt me

In this instance the minister is very selective about what he or she presents, or is passive and reticent. The appraisal falls down because insufficient information is shared to enable detailed examination of the minister's work.

Ministry à trois

'Now you've heard all about my parish. What priorities would you have in my position?' asks the minister of the appraiser. 'And what else would you suggest?' asks the minister, off-loading the responsibility for analysis and decision-making onto the consultant. Since it is part of the appraiser's task to offer an analysis, and perhaps at times to make suggestions, it is tempting for the appraiser to hook into this, and to seize on all the openings provided to act the capable parent to the dependent child.

I did like you told me

This game is the next instalment of the above, where the minister returns for the next appraisal having applied the consultant's advice in what Kadushin calls 'spiteful obedience'. He or she then acts as if the consultant were now responsible for the work. The appraised minister appears to be just the executor of the appraiser's directives.

Kadushin also lists some games which supervisors (and presumably appraisers) can play, masking the consultant's lack of knowledge or understanding on the one hand, or lack of evidence or assertions on the other. They need not be spelled out in any more detail here. Kadushin accepts that the games he described are caricatures. Nonetheless they contain selective but essentially accurate aspects of the supervisory relationship which have relevance too in the way in which appraisal is responded to by minister and consultant. The way to avoid these games is to decline to play them and to deny oneself 'the sweet fruits of flattery, the joys of omniscience, the pleasures of acting the therapist, the gratification of being liked.'[7] As in counselling and supervision the appraiser can confront any of the games in three ways: firstly through being sensitive to the minister's anxieties about appraisal; secondly through helping him or her to overcome, as much as is possible, the embarrassment, discomfort and threat which appraisal arouses; and thirdly through inviting the minister to make a more open assessment of actual situations which are being avoided or glossed over.

The requirements of the appraiser

Clearly the role of the appraiser or consultant is a vital one, given the concerns that some ministers will have at the prospect of appraisal. It is because the consultant is such a key person in the success or failure of an appraisal scheme that I concentrate first upon the necessary skills and insights required for appraisal interviewing, before looking in the next chapter at a form of appraisal that might be used.

A group of clergy in one diocese were asked what characteristics they would want in a consultant to assist them with their own self-appraisal. Their answers included:

> someone who is sympathetic and likes me,
> yet someone also at the right critical distance,
> and one who is sufficiently detached;
> someone discerning, wise and insightful,
> who relates adult to adult,
> who does not become an authority figure,
> yet who shows expertise and is able to ask the right questions;
> someone who is able to use my language,
> and who is knowledgeable about the situation I am in;
> someone who is adaptable, and trustworthy,
> who can hold confidences, and is on the level;
> someone who hurts only in order to heal;
> who has their own consultant for self-appraisal;
> who is a sounding board, with a sense of humour;
> someone who can accept payment.

Such a person is clearly worth paying for!

Various authors have listed the skills required of the person conducting appraisal. Nelson lists them as the four skills of analysis, communication, counselling and organisation.[8] He also lists four qualities of the structured approach that is needed in the consultants:[9]

a. *contact*: they should be able to help the appraised person to feel at ease, relaxed, and assured of their full and undivided attention;

b. *control*: they can use the time to achieve its purpose, structuring it to reach what Nelson calls 'agreed improvement objectives';

c. *content*: their approach should be relevant and comprehensive;

d. *conversational skill*: they need to listen carefully, asking questions in a non-judgemental way.

The skills of listening and responding are frequently referred to by authors writing about the conduct of appraisal interviews. I have written about such skills in detail in another book in this series.[10] Management trainers similarly stress the need to listen; the use of open questions, rather than closed, loaded or multiple questions; and the need to avoid talking too much, interrupting too often, and getting caught up in arguments.

In addition to the cultivation of these more passive skills in appraisal interviewing, it is equally important in appraising to learn other more active skills, which will be used in order to intervene where necessary to make the best use of the time and opportunity available. As I have already suggested above, a consultant needs to learn how to open areas up quickly and yet delicately, and to confront sufficiently strongly to explore difficulties, without being so blunt that open wounds are left bleeding at the end of the interview.

These are not easy skills to acquire. It is reassuring to find Randell et al. describing problems which managers have in appraising.[11] They list some of the difficulties which managers have when it is necessary to conduct an appraisal of an employee whose performance is unsatisfactory. There are clearly appraiser's games which run parallel to those listed by Kadushin above, since they mention managers who conduct difficult interviews informally, strolling round the car park, or over lunch. They may be hesitant about opening up some areas for discussion, particularly when they have to be critical. The example is given of a manager who walked an employee back and forth past a tailor's shop, pausing each time to look in the window; it was only on the sixth stop that the employee realized that a big hint was being dropped about his own style of dress![12]

Other common difficulties experienced by appraisers include problems in systematically pursuing points, in moving on to firm recommendations or actions where a person might improve, of defending the organization when the appraised person is critical of it, and of abandoning useful topics just when they are getting to the nub of a problem.

Trasler[13] illustrates the difference between two types of

appraisal interview, the controlling and the developmental, by pointing to the way these are reflected in the style of an appraiser's interventions:

controlling interventions	*developmental interventions*
I think my suggestions are clear, so why don't you get back to work?	Let's think about these possibilities and get back together next week after you've thought about them.
You've got a problem there.	We've got a problem here.

Randell et al. also distinguish different types of interview, each with its own style of interviewing. Although some of these may not appear immediately relevant to clergy appraisal, we should not forget that some interviews in church life, whether of ministers or by ministers, may involve telling people things that they do not want to hear, which the appraiser would prefer not to have to communicate, but which someone has to say:

a. *the 'tell-sell' interview*, conducted with people who are unwilling to take a developmental step. It should be short, sharp and purposeful. The trouble with it is that the subject may not agree but does not say so, and so leaves the interview and does nothing about it.

b. *the 'tell-listen' interview*, where there is the need to say some things but the subject is full of ideas too. The manager suggests a line of action, but listens to the subject to see how it might be pursued.

c. *the 'listen-support' interview*, used especially when the subject is experiencing frustration, alienation or conflict. This is similar to a counselling interview. It is time-consuming, but when the need for it occurs all other demands of the interview are dropped.

d. *grievance interviews*, where the interviewer needs to do most of the listening.

e. *separation interviews*, where it is necessary to dismiss the subject; this is a combination of 'tell-sell-listen-support', concluding with goal setting.

The skills and qualities required of appraisers, as described in management training, need to be supplemented by particular knowledge of the organization and the context in which appraisal takes place. In their report on appraisal and assessment, Hiscox et al.[14] suggest that the expertise of appraisal interviewers should include:

1. an understanding of communities and the dynamics of community life;
2. an understanding of parishes and the dynamics of parish life;
3. an awareness of the differences between communities and parishes within a diocese;
4. an awareness of possible differences of values and a readiness to explore the minister's values rather than to impose one's own;
5. the ability to help people to analyse and think through their situation, and to reflect back the implications of what they are saying and doing so that they see it in a new way;
6. a willingness to help the minister to identify and explore significant issues, to struggle with their complexity and to set long-term goals and short-term objectives as and when appropriate;
7. a knowledge of the human and material resources available in the diocese and beyond,[15] so that the ministerial review is followed by appropriate action and further training.

Although there is obviously value in the knowledge suggested in the first three items, my own stress would be on the qualities and skills described in points 4, 5 and 6, and on the knowledge of resources in point 7.

Planning and assessing the appraisal interview

Just as the minister being appraised needs an opportunity to prepare for appraisal, as I shall examine in more detail in the next chapter, so the consultant in the process needs to think about the structure of the interview. Randell et al. provide some helpful advice, particularly when they warn against attempting too much in one interview. They spell out four clear principles:

keep it simple;
don't attempt too much;
observe and record behaviours rather than personality;
build in capacity for change and development.[16]

They outline three stages to the appraisal interview, which, adapted to a church setting, involve:

1. gathering information: the minister gives an account of her or his work, or of some part of it; the consultant draws out sufficient information to proceed to the second stage of the interview; where the appraiser is a bishop or other senior cleric, this part of the interview also provides an opportunity to check out staff perceptions of a minister with the minister's self-perception.
2. identifying an area for development and growth. Randell et al. indicate that at this point the appraiser decides which of the different strategies outlined earlier to use (i.e. tell-sell-listen-support).
3. the final stage, which includes summing up, agreeing conclusions and planning the next step. This is the only stage, they suggest, when notes need to be taken, so that the conclusions of the interview are clear to both parties; this assists them to take up progress on the clarified objectives when they next meet.

These authors, even though they write on appraisal in the context of commerce and industry, suggest that the only report that needs to be made is that the meeting has taken place. If the organization insists on a report being filed, then it must be countersigned by the subject.

Following the appraisal interview, Randell et al. recommend that the meeting is reviewed. What might the consultant have done differently? What has he or she learned about his or her own skill in interviewing from the interview? Did the opening put the subject at ease? Did it raise anxiety? Was it formal or casual? In the middle section was the interviewer sensitive to the subject's feelings, listening, using good or bad techniques to question, following a purposeful path, making objectives clear, varying the pace? Was there rapport, an inclination to agree? Who dominated the interview? When it came to finishing the interview how was the subject left: high, low, sullen, content, motivated, crushed or rejecting the appraisal? Was the appraisal a step forwards or backwards or a non-event? All these are particularly valuable questions to use in training consultants, but also in reflection after an appraisal interview.

Randell and his colleagues have researched the perceptions on both sides of how an interview has gone, and have found wide differences in the way in which appraiser and appraised view what happened. They include an interview analysis form,[17] which can be used in training consultants, but could also be used for feedback in appraisal itself. My own adapted version of this appears opposite. The square brackets indicate alternative wording for a second version of the analysis form which can be completed by the appraiser, so that a comparison can be made between the perceptions of both parties. In appraisal schemes the appraised minister's responses can be sent to an independent third party, for comparison with the appraiser's analysis. Where one consultant conducts several appraisals, this third party can feed back a general picture of how the interviews were perceived on both sides. If the appraiser is only involved in one or two such interviews, careful use needs to be made of the information, unless both sides are happy that their appraisal analysis can be shared with each other.

Appraisal of appraisal may feel like wheels within wheels. Yet if those who agree to be appraised know that their consultants also seek feedback on their work as appraisers as well as on their own ministry, this increases the trust and honesty of those who put their ministry in the hands of those who can help them review it. The professional approach to consultancy that has been taken in this chapter is an indication of the seriousness with which the task needs to be undertaken, since appraisal is more than work consultancy. Appraisal is also a step in the direction of 'that openness to

APPRAISAL ANALYSIS

Appraiser's name:
Appraised's name:

1. How satisfied were you with the appraiser's [*appraised person's*] response to you during the appraisal? (Ring the appropriate point on the scale, 1. if you were 'very dissatisfied', 6. if you were 'very satisfied', etc.)

very dissatisfied   1   2   3   4   5   6   very satisfied

2. Ring on each scale which number best describes the appraiser's [*appraised person's*] behaviour:

followed his or her [*my*] agenda	1	2	3	4	5	6	followed my [*his/her*] agenda
undermining	1	2	3	4	5	6	supporting
frank/honest	1	2	3	4	5	6	reticent
listening	1	2	3	4	5	6	talking
indifferent	1	2	3	4	5	6	concerned

3. If as a result of the appraisal the appraiser [*you*] or you [*the person appraised*] agreed on certain aims or actions, please list them:

   what the appraiser [/] agreed to do

   what I [*the appraised person*] agreed to do

4. How satisfied were you with the appraisal overall:

very satisfied   1   2   3   4   5   6   very dissatisfied

God [which] brings about a deep seated remaking of a person . . . a process of gradually facing more and more of the truth about ourselves so that eventually the whole of our personalities are rooted and grounded in God and his love.'[18]

Notes

1. B. Hartung, 'The capacity to enter latency in learning pastoral psychotherapy'. *Journal of Supervision and Training in Ministry*, vol. 2, Chicago, Illinois, 1979.
2. M. Jacobs, *The Presenting Past*. Open University Press 1986.
3. B. Hartung, 'The capacity to enter latency', p. 47.
4. H. Searles, 'Problems of Psycho-analytic Supervision'. *Collected Papers on Schizophrenia and Related Subjects*, Hogarth Press 1965.
5. J. Foskett and D. Lyall, *Helping the Helpers*. SPCK 1988, pp. 119–122. The whole of Chapter 8 provides valuable insights into the learning relationship which are equally applicable to appraisal.
6. A. Kadushin, 'Games People Play in Supervision'. *Social Work* (USA), 13:3, 1968, pp. 23–32.
7. ibid., p. 32.
8. J. Mills and J. Nelson, eds, *Explorations into Parish Ministry: a Guide to Joint Work Consultation*. Diocese of Liverpool 1983, p. 21.
9. ibid., p. 27.
10. M. Jacobs, *Swift to Hear*. SPCK 1985.
11. G. Randell, P. Packard and J. Slater, *Staff Appraisal*. Institute of Personnel Management, 3rd edn 1984.
12. ibid., p. 54.
13. J. Trasler, *Performance Appraisal*. The Council for Education and Training in Youth and Community Work, p. 22.
14. R. Hiscox, J. Gammell and C. Raybould, *Report of the Working Group on Appraisal and Assessment*. Church of England Continuing Ministerial Education Committee, May 1988, p. 9.
15. In connection with this item, a valuable resource book for both the appraiser and the appraised is the *Directory of Training Opportunities for the Clergy* published every two years by ACCM, Church House, Great Smith Street, London SW1P 3NZ.
16. G. Randell et al., *Staff Appraisal*, p. 37.
17. ibid., p. 75.
18. R. P. Reiss, in an appendix to an ACCM report on the psychological assessment of candidates, 1979.

SEVEN

Specific Suggestions

In the appraisal of ministry there are certain principles which need to be attended to, procedures which need clarifying, and areas for consideration which need to be addressed. This is true whether the form of appraisal agreed upon in a church organization, province or diocese is that it should be universally applied to all ministers, or offered as a valuable option; whether a minister has to find her or his own consultant for appraisal, or is asked to see a particular person: whatever conclusions on these questions are reached.

In accordance with my approach throughout, I do not presume to make strong recommendations one way or another, but aim to set out the possibilities. In this chapter I look at factors to be borne in mind in the arrangements for appraisal: the areas which could be covered in the meeting with the consultant (or in self- or peer appraisal) and a form of peer appraisal for use in small groups. Whereas in the last chapter I had the appraiser or consultant mainly in mind, here I focus on the minister who has chosen, or been asked, to appraise her or his ministry.

Arrangements for appraisal[1]

Those being appraised need to know the purpose of appraisal, as well as its boundaries. If it is to be about performance and accountability to the employing authority, it will need to be conducted by someone with institutional authority and may be expected to be compulsory. If it is to be about work alone, that is one thing; but if it is intended that it should include personal development, then it probably needs either to be voluntary or at least to be conducted by someone of the individual's own choosing, perhaps from a panel of selected and trained consultants. If it is voluntary it needs to be made clear that there is no covert or overt disapproval of those who refuse to take part in the scheme. It needs to be clear whether the employing institution is to be told any or all of the results of the interview. All these factors must be known to all parties before any agreement is made to take part in appraisal.

It is important where there is a choice of appraiser to exercise care in choosing someone who will fulfil some of the requirements of a consultant described in the last chapter. If the scheme is promoted by a diocese, district or province, then a list of consultants should be made available. An initial meeting may be arranged, but with no contract to meet agreed until both parties have had the chance to get to know each other's style, as well as their underlying assumptions and values. If each of them has a different view of mission, for example, the appraisal process is unlikely to be of much help to either. If it does not appear that the appraiser initially approached is the right person, it is much better to say so and to look again, than to press on half-heartedly or to give up and do no more about it.

When consultant and minister feel they can work together, they then need to agree the time and place of meeting, the length of the interview, and the frequency of their meetings. I myself believe that every six months is not too frequent, given the diverse responsibilities involved in most ministries and the time it takes to look at any one area at a meeting. A meeting of less than an hour and a half provides insufficient time, although too extended a meeting could also prove less productive in proportion to the time expended. In some cases it will also be necessary to agree on financial matters: who pays the consultant? who pays the expenses involved? Where the meetings take place is also an important question: there may be value in the consultant seeing the parochial situation at first hand; or it may be just as important for the minister to be out of the work location for the appraisal meeting, with someone and somewhere neutral. There is no harm in all these very practical arrangements being written down and agreed, not in the form of a legal contract, but as a clear statement of the arrangements between two people.

Consultant and minister can usefully spend a preliminary session reaching common understanding of the minister's situation. This may be largely factual, involving perhaps the completion of a profile of the parish or local church, or sharing the results of a parish audit if this has been done (see Chapter 9). It is important that both agree on their understanding of the particular minister's task. This may be an opportunity to draw up a job description (see Chapter 5) if one does not exist already.

Before each session the person being appraised needs to take time to think about her or his ministry, and which aspects could most usefully be discussed. The agenda for appraisal below provides a long enough list of questions to keep meetings going for years; it is important that not too much is attempted at one session. Those preparing for appraisal may wish to take soundings from colleagues or church members on particular areas of their ministry, so that they can share this information with their consultant and check their self-perception. After the first appraisal has taken place, an important aspect of the immediate preparation for subsequent appraisals is to remind oneself of the goals, objectives or action plan agreed with the consultant last time, and to assess how far these have been met.

Finally, as the session draws to a close, both consultant and appraised minister need to agree upon any follow-up, or what is sometimes called 'an action plan'. Given what has been talked about, and the ways ahead that might have been identified, what action can the minister take between now and the next appraisal to further development or change? It may be useful for this to be written down at the time and agreed between the two. Following the meeting the consultant can write to the minister outlining her or his main conclusions from their time together and asking that these should be confirmed or refined by the person who came for appraisal. The consultant may also agree to follow up the interview, for instance by taking up an issue with someone in authority in the institution; this needs to be done in writing, with copies to the minister. Alternatively the consultant may undertake to get information which will help the appraised to approach the right people for help with training and development, etc.

Each party needs to be sure of what the other is doing in the way of follow-up, so that the initiatives agreed do not get lost. It is vital that any information coming from the appraisal which needs to be shared outside is agreed by the minister who has been appraised. If a report is to be sent on to another person, then this must be agreed and signed by both parties, with the opportunity for a dissenting statement to be made by either if they cannot agree. It may be valuable for each to write a summary of the session and send it to the other. Any such arrangements as these will have been agreed at the preliminary meeting.

Agenda for appraisal

A week before the date for appraisal, the minister and the consultant each need to find time to read through the questions suggested in the appraisal procedure. Most schemes produce a fairly detailed list of areas to think about, or questions to answer. In this section I include as many of those questions as possible, with a view to providing a comprehensive collection of foci for appraisal, but with no intention that they all should be tackled at one sitting. Not all of them will be relevant, and there may well be other questions which the minister or the consultant want to add.

My own preference is for the appraised person to set the agenda, and to select those areas which he or she wishes to raise with the consultant. However, since the consultant has had the chance to read through the same list of topics, the consultant may from time to time raise an area which seems important, and which may even be notable by its absence from the minister's self-appraisal. But if the consultant's questions seem irrelevant, then the minister should say so.

Questions that might be addressed in self-appraisal or in preparation for appraisal with a consultant

A. The setting for your ministry[2]
(*This section can be drawn up for the first appraisal, and at each change of post, but need only be updated annually thereafter*)

1. To whom are you responsible? How often do you see them, and what is your relationship with them?

2. For whom and what are you responsible? Use your job description here, or use this as an opportunity to draft one. Are there any major changes in your responsibilities since you were appointed, or since your last appraisal, which need to be included?

3. Staffing in your local church, including non-stipendiary ministers, readers etc.

4. Churches in your ministry: church membership, description of social mix of the congregation(s), ages, number of children, elderly, etc.

5. Worship: services you are responsible for, on Sundays, weekdays, number of baptisms, marriages, funerals per annum.

6. Church organizations: Sunday schools, youth clubs, uniformed, etc.

7. Communications: magazines, newsletters, contact with local broadcasting networks, press, etc.

8. Description of area: social structure of population, ethnic groups, schools, community centres, industry and commerce, hospitals and other institutions.

9. Community concerns, particularly issues over the last twelve months; how far have you or your church been involved in these?

10. Other denominations in the locality: ecumenical relationships.

11. What are the specific needs of the situation (church and local community) in which you work? What are the present priorities?

B. Your current ministry
(*For second and subsequent appraisals question 12 is essential. But do not attempt to tackle too many of the other questions in one appraisal. Leave time for question C.26 and review of the appraisal as suggested in D.32*)

12. Since you last met your consultant, how far have the objectives you set then been realized?

How far have you been able to move in resolving any of the difficulties you mentioned at that time?

What factors have contributed to any achievement of your objectives?

What factors have hindered the achievement of your objectives?

13. The following areas cover the major part of a person's ministry, but you may want to add other areas to the list as you review your own. The various terms will, of course, mean different things to different people. Clarify with your consultant if you are unsure whether you both mean the same thing:

Worship	Evangelism	Education (Children and Young People)
Administration	Finance	Adult Education
Pastoral Work	Family Life	Ecumenical Relations
Personal Development	Theology	Social and Community Concern[3]

14. Describe what you do from day to day, week to week.

What proportion of time do different activities take?

Would you wish to give more time to some, and less time to other activities?

Is it possible to make changes to help you do this?

15. What do you most like doing in your ministry?

What single occasion since the last appraisal has given you the most pleasure in your ministry?

What factors in the situation or in yourself contributed to that occasion?

What are your particular strengths?

Have you got skills and strengths you are not using in your ministry?

For second and subsequent meetings:

What particular part of your ministry has developed since your last appraisal?

16. What do you least like doing?

What single occasion since the last appraisal gave you the most dissatisfaction in your ministry?

What factors in the situation or in yourself contributed to this occasion?

What are you not particularly good at?

Does this mean you should consider involving someone else in those responsibilities?

Is what you like doing connected with how well you can do it?

Or is what you least like doing connected with what you find difficult?

If this is the case, is there any means of gaining more confidence in those aspects of ministry you feel doubtful about?

17. What means do you have of getting feedback from other people — family, colleagues, those to whom you minister?

What sort of feedback do you get about different aspects of your ministry?

How do you react to criticism or praise?

18. What do others expect of you in your work — the parish, the diocese, etc?

What do you expect of yourself? How do you measure 'success'?

19. How do you get on with other people who share in your ministry — readers, lay leaders, other clergy in the parish or deanery?

What are your expectations of them?

Are those expectations being fulfilled or frustrated?

How would you like to see working relationships develop?

Are there any particular strains in working or personal relationships that could usefully be talked about confidentially in your appraisal?

How do you get on with diocesan officers, senior clergy, the bishop and his staff, etc.?

Do you think they have a fair impression of you?

20. What other groups do you belong to outside your main line of duty — church and non-church?

What do you gain from your membership of them?

How does your membership of them help your main responsibilities?

How does the church gain?

21. How are you affected by changes in thinking in society around you, and in the church?

Do you have the opportunity to read and to discuss ideas freely with people who are not shocked by the questions that you may want to ask?

Have you attended any training courses or study days since your last appraisal?

In what other ways have you tried to increase your knowledge and experience since the last appraisal?

22. What time do you have for yourself and your family and/or friends?

What are your and their interests outside church life?

What is your health like, and also that of your family?

Do you need more time off?

Do you need to develop ways of 'getting away from the job'—recreation, outside interests, etc.?

What goals might be usefully set for these other aspects of your life?

23. You may want to talk about the very practical aspects of your situation: finance, accommodation, etc., especially if any of these 'external' factors could be adding unnecessary strain to your family life and to your ministry.

24. Your consultant is not a spiritual director, but you may like to think about the opportunity to develop this side of your life in your ministry.

What does spirituality mean to you? (never mind what it appears to mean to others.)

How have your thinking and your spiritual life grown and developed in relation to your beliefs and values?

How might you develop these personal spiritual dimensions (as you define them) in your ministry, particularly for yourself, but perhaps also in others (as their spiritual guide)?

Do you have a spiritual director, soul friend, or similar resource?

25. Are there any other areas of your present ministry you want to discuss?

C. Developing your ministry into the future

26. Do you have definite objectives for next year?

What would you like to achieve in the next year?

Are your goals realistic?

What plans do you have for action following this appraisal, and before the next?

[Ensure that you record your decision about this when you have your appraisal, and that you refer back to it when considering question B.12 at the next appraisal.]

27. Would training in any particular direction help you to achieve the above objectives?

28. What are the obstacles to the development of your ministry? Do they lie in resources (other people, finance, plant), in the organization or institution (the way the church is run) or in yourself (attitudes, skills, knowledge, motivation, personality)?

29. How long have you been in your present post?

When do you see yourself moving on?

What specific training or experience would be valuable for your long-term development in ministry?

30. Do you want to look further ahead than a year to how you want or expect your ministry to be in five years' time?

What would you like to be doing then?

Is there any way this might come about?

What do you need to be doing *now* to help effect that type of change?

D. Conclusion

31. What areas of your ministry have you not talked about?

Is it because they are irrelevant or unimportant or because you are not yet confident about discussing them?

Are there any other items you want to discuss next time, which you wish to 'flag up' now?

32. Has the appraisal been helpful?

In what way could it have been more helpful?

Have you and your consultant got any suggestion at this point for improvements in the way you both go about it next time?

When are you next going to meet?

Appraisal for readers, local preachers and lay ministers

It is a measure of just how extensive lay ministry is that the majority of the questions listed above apply equally to those who serve the Church in their 'spare time' as readers, local preachers, churchwardens, stewards, leaders of organizations, etc. Whether appraisal is a valuable exercise for these ministers must be a matter for local decision. In my own work with readers in one diocese it was clear that there was a greater interest in annual appraisal of their own ministry than had been apparent amongst clergy. Part of their reason may have been some frustration with the ways in which they were used or not used, and they may have seen appraisal (quite appropriately) as a way of raising these issues.

Nevertheless some of the questions and perhaps even the method needs adaptation. It would seem appropriate that appraisal is conducted by the ordained minister to whom the lay minister is responsible: readers should ideally see their incumbents, or local preachers their local minister, although arrangements need to be made for those instances where there are personal factors on either side blocking useful communication. So too I would think it important that junior clergy in training (and maybe bishop's staffs) should have their appraisal with the man or woman to whom they are responsible and who knows their work best. Whereas most ordained ministers work in situations where they have infrequent contact with senior clergy in the Church, and therefore can validly seek appraisal from an independent consultant, there are some clergy (the most junior and the more senior) who have clearer lines of responsibility, and who might be more usefully appraised by those with whom they work closely and to whom they are directly answerable.

Those who wish to use appraisal with lay ministers and with other lay employees of the local church will need to make their own adaptation of the questions listed above, preferably inviting the co-operation of those who agree to the appraisal procedure. I suggest that Section A on the setting for ministry will probably not be needed and that recognition is given in Section B to the more limited time which most lay ministers have to offer. Nevertheless, the questions provide a way of extending the vision of lay ministry. Question B.13, for example, lists more areas which may be applicable to a lay minister's ministry than are normally considered. Here the question (in this instance adapted for a reader) might be phrased:

13. The following areas might be part of a reader's ministry. Select those areas which apply to you, and bear them in mind as you address the later questions. Ignore those areas which are not part of your reader's ministry unless you would like them to be so.

Worship	Evangelism	Education (Children and Young People)
Administration	Finance	Adult Education
Pastoral Work	Family Life	Ecumenical Relations
Personal Development	Theology	Social and Community Concern

List your responsibilities in the areas you have selected.
How much of your time do they take up?
Do your activities take up too much of your time, or do you feel you are not being used enough?
Would you wish to give more time to some activities, and less time to others?
Is it possible to make changes to help you do this?

Since lay ministers (unlike ordained ministers) should not have the same need to carry out responsibilities which they are not good at and therefore do not necessarily need help to improve their skills in some areas of ministry, some questions can be phrased to allow choices. For example, question B.15 might be rewritten as:

15. What do you least like doing as a reader?
What single occasion gave you the most dissatisfaction as a reader during the last year?
What are you not particularly good at?
Does this mean you should drop those aspects or are there ways of helping you to feel happier about them?

Other obvious examples of the need to adapt the questions are:

19. How do you get on with people who share in the ministry of your parish — clergy, churchwardens or stewards, church council members, choir and servers, lay leaders, other readers?
How would you like to see working relationships develop?
Are there any particular strains in working or personal relationships that could usefully be talked about confidentially in your appraisal?
22. How about time for yourself, and your family and/or friends?
What are your and their interests outside church life?
Do you need some regular time off to let you become an 'ordinary worshipper'?
Does being a reader affect your working life in any valuable or adverse way?
23. Are there any practical matters you need to raise, such as out of pocket expenses, service rosters, advance notice of engagements, etc.?
Are there any minor or major irritations about your ministry which put an unnecessary strain on it?

A form of peer appraisal

In the last chapter I look at ways of extending appraisal and review to wider aspects of church life. Although the following account of peer appraisal could as easily stand in that chapter as an example of the way in which a group can assess levels of achievement of its tasks, the method described also has value in the design and application of appraisal procedures. Where a group of ministers lack the framework of any scheme provided by their church, or where they wish to carry through a particular piece of personal or task assessment, the methods suggested by James Kilty are of considerable value.[4] While the suggestions already made in this chapter can provide some ideas for such a group, the method essentially encourages them to develop their own method of appraisal.

In his paper on peer assessment or peer audit Kilty outlines twelve or more steps in the design and application of appraisal. How far the peers go in assisting each other depends on the level of trust in the group. Essentially he describes two parts to the exercise: design (1—4) and application (5—13). Some groups may only go as far as the first part, leaving application to individuals or pairs. I shall give examples below of how this method might be used in group and team ministries, by ecumenical groups, or by church councils and other policy making groups, for the type of reviews and research projects referred to in Chapter 9. In the latter case both design of the assessment and its application will normally be used.

The steps which Kilty suggests are as follows. A facilitator might be useful to the group in its working through some of these:

1. The small group brainstorms in order to select the area of concern which members might want to assess. Since the group has limited time for this exercise, selection of one clearly defined aspect seems sensible. Or following the brainstorming the facilitator may suggest an area to assess.

appraisal example: to assess how far personal qualities affect competence in pastoral work.

research project: to assess the effect of differing baptismal policies in the area.

2. The group agree their criteria for competent practice, i.e. what will be valid indicators of success or failure. These may include readily quanitifiable data, so that the peer group can engage in its own mini-research project; or they may be much more subjective.

appraisal example: the criteria adopted are levels of empathy, warmth and acceptance.

research project: the criteria adopted are subsequent church attendance by the families affected by different policies and their subsequent attitude to the Church.

3. They then agree methods to assess these criteria, which will range from subjective self-assessment, to number-crunching through records, questionnaires, etc.

appraisal example: members of the group will ask others in the group to rate them on a list of personal qualities.

research project: record of attendance for one year following baptism, and informal interview (but with standard questions) of family six months after initial enquiry.

4. The group then discusses how findings can be applied in a practical way.

appraisal example: human relations training where necessary.

research project: review of baptismal policies, or of the way they are communicated to families.

Kilty suggests that some groups will want to stop at this point. The members have helped each other to determine a way of assessing a situation and each person then proceeds to make their own assessment, or each church carries through its own piece of research. However, for research purposes (particularly in the example given) it seems foolish to stop at that point, since the pooling of information and results is essential. In design of an appraisal procedure, the group may then split into pairs and come back to review the exercise at a later date. But Kilty suggests that the group can also be used for actual peer appraisal.

5. The group meet to consider how far each has been able to apply the agreed procedure and to look at what barriers there may have been to its implementation. For example one church may have decided they felt that the action of the Holy Spirit was being doubted and they had reservations about conducting research into a baptism policy, which had been adopted after much prayer. Another church may have found it difficult to find interviewers.

6. The group members share the results of their work. If a piece of mini-research has been carried out this may not be too difficult; but the disclosure of more personal assessment will need encouragement and support. The freedom of group members not to disclose personal matters must be emphasized. Those who do not want to report need not. During the reporting the rest of the group listen, but do not intervene.

Again, some groups prefer to stop here (especially if the project is an aspect of personal assessment), although it would be possible to move to step 10 by omitting steps 7, 8 and 9 if these were felt to be too difficult. Steps 6–10 might also be done in pairs, with equal time given to each partner, rather than in a group setting, to reduce anxiety.

7. This step involves discreet questioning and clarification of the findings or the assessment, either by the partner (if in pairs) or in the group.

8. This step involves peer assessment: here the members of the peer group are invited to respond if they so wish, and express support but also disagreement. For steps 7−9 to be effective the group members and the facilitator require good interpersonal skills in both group members and facilitator. The nature of this feedback needs to be kept clearly personal, i.e. 'This is my opinion . . . I feel . . .' since some of the feedback will have doubtful validity, and some will consist of positive or negative projections.

9. A step which draws upon the idea of the devil's advocate: it is more challenging, including amplification of any of the doubts the peers may have about aspects of a colleague's competence, or about research findings. It is this part which demands the greatest skill; when personal matters are under review it can only be used in groups where there is a high level of trust.

10. Having highlighted negative elements the next step highlights strengths, and consists of the sharing of positive impressions of a person's competence, especially if these have not previously been acknowledged.

11. This stage consists of review of the appraisal, or the research and its results, as well as the feedback. It is essentially both a summing-up of the previous steps and of action planned.

12. The last or penultimate step is to review the procedure that has been used in steps 1−11, to revise the criteria and methods in the light of the findings. It may, for example, be felt that there is as yet insufficient statistical evidence that a particular baptism policy works better than another, and that the interviewing of families needs to take place for a further year to get a better sample.

13. This final step is only applicable to less personal aspects of appraisal and to mini-research projects, since it involves

the communication of the results of the project to other groups or individuals and even to a wider audience.

This chapter has outlined some suggestions for methods and content of the appraisal procedure. What the appraiser and appraised person may find emerging as a result of an open and honest meeting may be a surprise (and even a pleasure) to both. In the next chapter I look at some of the satisfactions and stresses that may be shared in an appraisal.

Notes

1. This section draws partly on a privately circulated paper written by R. P. Reiss, dated 1982.
2. This section on setting owes much to the scheme developed in the Diocese of Coventry by the Revd Clive Raybould.
3. These areas of ministry are drawn from J. Mills and J. Nelson, eds, *Explorations into Parish Ministry: a Guide to Joint Work Consultation.* Diocese of Liverpool 1983.
4. J. Kilty, *Self and Peer Assessment and Peer Audit.* Human Potential Research Project, University of Surrey, 1979.

EIGHT

Attraction and Alienation

Feedback

The discussion of work and practice which takes place in appraisal is private, and few people other than the consultant will know what any one person says to another, except in those cases where reports of appraisal are sent to and shared between the most senior level of clergy. Nevertheless there are three ways in which the information which comes from a series of appraisals with different individuals can be of value. Firstly, it will be important feedback for the employing church, providing information which a sensitive employer will be able to use in better meeting the needs of the ministers. Secondly, the accumulated knowledge which a consultant builds up over a number of appraisals will enable her or him not only to understand more about any one individual, but will also enable the consultant to draw upon the understanding of strains and rewards described to single out areas of concern as they arise in the course of any single appraisal. For instance, a consultant may detect concern about confidentiality after the first one or two appraisals; he or she will then be more alert to this issue in seeing those who have yet to come for their first appraisal. Thirdly, the information which comes from appraisal can also be beneficial and supportive for individual ministers themselves, not least because the picture of ministry which is built up will often help them to feel less isolated and unusual: they become aware that others often feel the same.

The difficulty is how this information can be shared in such a way as to increase the understanding of the employing church or to convey supportive knowledge to individual ministers, without at the same time divulging personal information. While wishing to sustain the utmost confidentiality, it would be a pity for such accumulated knowledge to remain private, only of use to the consultant, and therefore only indirectly helpful to those whom the consultant assists. If only such knowledge about ministry could be pooled, by disguising it, generalizing it and diluting it amidst a wealth of feedback so that no individual can be identified, there is much that could be learned.

As part of the Ministry to Priests Programme (described in Chapter 4) a comprehensive report is produced for the Roman Catholic diocese, which draws upon the data gathered from the series of interviews conducted with its priests. These reports are confidential and I cannot use them here, except to point out in a general way how answers to a question such as 'What would help the priests to live a fuller spiritual life?' are reproduced under a series of headings: spiritual needs, needs for the self in relationship to others, community and social needs, health needs and work needs. A large number of suggestions and ideas from these interviews are conveyed, without any identification of the individuals who put them forward. This provides a sketch of a typical priest's needs. Furnished with such information, those who have responsibility for the continuation of the Ministry to Priests Programme can attempt to provide for some of those needs through training of all kinds, through adjustments to working conditions and through promoting more support and care by the diocese and by fellow priests.

In the general absence of publishable information from appraisal schemes themselves about the needs, joys and stresses encountered in ministry I can partially supply this lack by drawing upon the answers to questions posed by myself to clergy in parish and sector ministry, and to Church of England readers about the satisfactions and frustrations of their work. Later in the chapter I also summarize some of the literature on stress and burnout, so that consultants and individual ministers using appraisal will have some pointers with which to understand better what is expressed in the course of their meeting.[1]

The attractions and frustrations of ministry

Pryor,[2] in his research in Victoria, Australia, found that the activities which ministers disliked most were managing the church office, records and correspondence, church meetings and planning and arranging programmes. The activities they enjoyed most were administering the sacraments, followed by leading worship, preaching, and helping individuals to Christian commitment. Amongst their current frustrations,[3] in rank order, were lack of opportunity to do specialized work or training, disillusionment with the Church's relevance to the modern world, improving the parish being seen as a hopeless task, and feeling inadequate as a minister and leader. Particular problems cited[4] were the workload, management of conflict, structures and procedures of the church, the expectations of the parishioners and delegating work. I only summarize the leading categories in each of these instances.

In a small pilot project I asked clergy of different denominations working in parishes and sector ministries, stipendiary and non-stipendiary, about their satisfactions and frustrations in ministry. Similar results emerge as in the Pryor study, although the fuller answers given enable finer understanding of what ministers find valuable and difficult.

Ministry involves many different tasks, and I asked my respondents which they identified as the most important ones in their own ministry. Counselling and pastoral work scored high (just over 50% included it), with leading worship second (just over 25%). There was more than one reference in the small sample to preaching, spiritual direction, training or teaching, and personal prayer and reflection. Other priorities mentioned were leading the church community into new experiences, creative expression through art and music, the promotion of lay responsibility and, in the case of one NSM, the importance of doing his 'secular' job well.

When asked what at the end of any day might have given them the greatest feelings of satisfaction, the most frequently mentioned response was a meeting or contact with someone, perhaps one in which they had seen someone grow in insight, or in understanding. This was followed by several references to the satisfaction of successfully completing a task, and being in control of the workload. The third largest source of satisfaction came from having met someone's need or in some way helping them. In relation to appraisal these findings are of some interest, since the second may be an area which can be looked at, in order to help a minister organize the working day realistically. But the greatest satisfaction, coming from a deep sense of having 'met' someone, is scarcely capable of realization through changing work patterns. It is partly to do with being more open as a person, but partly the result of those 'chance' meetings which are completely unpredictable, and certainly not capable of being engineered.

Other general satisfactions emerging from the respondents were being thanked, the variety of tasks in a day, the ability to see results, services that have gone well, personal and public prayer, the ability to organize work, being part of a team, a feeling of satisfaction in an NSM's secular work, a sense of order to the day and still having enough time for leisure at the end of it.

When asked more specifically to name the three most satisfying aspects of ministry, leading worship (as in Pryor's study) was at the top of the aspects mentioned, followed by counselling and pastoral contacts. Mention of the variety of tasks in ministry as being satisfying is perhaps borne out by the sheer variety of satisfactions which these ministers mentioned as experiencing in their work: fixing things, achieving something useful, challenging people further in their faith, enabling them to realize their gifts, sharing responsibility with the laity, seeing fresh insights or a sense of wonder dawn in people, celebrating the high moments of life, teaching, working in a team, knowing the people who come to church, contact with non-religious people, time to think, support and encouragement of friends, colleagues and others, involvement in church government, and personal theological development. Appraisal will no doubt draw out an equally rich list of satisfactions in ministry.

In response the general question about what might make them feel frustrated at the end of a day, the answers have no clear pattern, although the most common reference was to the feeling of mismatch or misunderstanding between self and another—to be expected as the opposite of the satisfaction of a real sense of meeting. Tasks which are left undone, or administration bogging the minister down also appear more than once. Amongst other (single) answers given were: the rejection of my ideas, not being appreciated, missing prayer or meditation, the gulf between self and nominal Christians, the lack of response, narrow evangelicalism or understanding of the faith, meetings where the conclusions are known beforehand, working at a superficial level, not challenging wrong assumptions, hearing difficulties which are intractable, conflict with some personalities. Notice the frequent references here to the failure to make real contact with other people, either because the people were themselves unwilling or because the minister felt unable to be more open. It is important to notice that appraisal will need to touch upon personal skills and qualities if it is to help the minister to tackle these types of frustrations. Although management of time may be necessary to assist with the more specific frustrations of ministry to do with time and administration, changing methods and priorities will not in themselves effect much change in the vital area (for both satisfaction and frustration) of making real contact with people through ministry.

The respondents were also asked to list the three most frustrating aspects of their ministry. Here the problems of time, administration, and lack of help and support from others in the church become much clearer. Trivial paperwork and administration are mentioned most frequently, as is sitting on committees, or concern with financial matters and fund-raising. The words 'lack of time' appear several times, either on their own or with reference to time for reading or for taking up opportunities, or too much time being spent organizing. Different types of church member cause frustration: the grumbling conservatives, those who want the minister to be cosy and paternalistic, those who show no insight or sense of outreach, the strong-willed who dominate, the boring, and the general laity who lack confidence. Some of the other frustrations mentioned are: the inability to communicate relevantly, the multiplicity of demands from the national Church, the inability to exercise a full ministry (said in different ways by a woman deacon and a male NSM), lack of involvement in planning, parochialism, folk religion, celibacy, and lack of resources.

In a different exercise, with a large group of Anglican readers, I also asked what were the most satisfying and frustrating features of their ministry. Since lay ministers make such an important contribution to church life and, as I suggested in Chapter 7, may have their own appraisal procedures, it is useful to compare and contrast their answers with those given by the clergy sample, although in the readers' case the statements came out of discussion groups, and no particular weighting can be attached to any single statement.

The most satisfying features of the readers' ministries were: relationships with others, being trusted, accepted, and approached; the discovery of self-worth; the wider fellowship, including that of readers as a whole; practical care such as transport; pastoral visiting and counselling (especially mentioned by women readers); the privilege of being allowed into people's lives and hearts; living with people in sorrows and joys; feeling part of God's plan; the deeper relationship with our Lord through discipline, prayer and study; preaching and the feedback from preaching, taking services and administering the chalice; the joy of preparing services; leading Bible studies and groups; being an authorized member of the church; being in the vanguard of change; and opportunities to serve God in the secular situation as well as in the 'holy'.

The most frustrating and difficult features of the readers' ministries were reported as follows: the incumbent/reader relationship, but also how the reader relates to others such as the churchwardens and other lay leaders; the lack of definition to the reader's role and therefore questions about it; fitting in with the church council; not having talents used properly and sufficiently; the lack of clear strategy for the use of readers; the lack of administration; the lack of opportunity to discuss ministry; expectations being sometimes too much; the lack of confidence in communication; the lack of human understanding in the parish; the lack of commitment by others; holding a neutral position in parish disputes; clashes of ideas and personalities; being sympathetic to differing Christian viewpoints in the parish; working within a team of different theological views; too much time spent in meetings on finance; church bureaucracy; lack of spirituality; lack of feedback and encouragement; destructive criticism; the anti-women movement in some churches; the demands of the family; lack of time to be oneself and alone, and finding time to do what one would like to do.

As in the case of the clergy the list of frustrations which the readers reported was longer than the list of satisfactions, but this should not in itself be taken as an indication of the balance between the attractions of ministry and the feelings of alienation. Although I come now to look at long-term stress and burnout, and therefore at potentially the most problematic areas of ministry that might arise in appraisal, it is very important to bear in mind the comment which was included on one of the clergy responses to my pilot survey, which typifies the tone of them all. This particular minister added a note: 'There are enormous satisfactions with just sufficient frustrations to keep me learning new approaches and new ways of coping.'

Alienation, stress and burnout

There is nothing wrong with stress as such. This point is made time and again in the literature on stress. It is, in its less damaging form, a set of physical and psychological reactions to immediate crises and forms a natural way of dealing with unexpected or emergency situations. It enables an individual to react to external stimuli through 'fight or flight', whichever is the most appropriate.

Ministry involves many situations which will induce this type of stress. What makes ministry so challenging is that there are few situations in pastoral work (for example) where stock answers can be given and easy solutions found. As one respondent to my survey commented, 'The good minister is at risk'. However, there are also other aspects of ministry which in time are more likely to sap energy than to stimulate it, and ministers themselves seem particularly prone to making a virtue out of the feelings of exhaustion produced by continuous stress. More than one book on stress in ministry quotes the prayer of Ignatius of Loyola, 'to give and not to count the cost . . . to toil and not to seek for rest', as being taken too literally by clergy.

It is long-term stress which gives rise to concern, since it is an indication that short-term stress has sapped energy to such an extent that the condition is more permanent; and instead of stress reactions heightening sensitivity to situations, stress becomes another sign of the burden of ministering to others. Amongst the signs of long-term stress are physical indicators such as exhaustion, tiredness which is not relieved by sleep, loss of energy, tearfulness, loss of interest in sex, slowing down, and other physical symptoms indicating a run-down condition. Mental responses include loss of creative vision, loss of perspective, poor judgement, muddled thinking, forgetfulness and indecision; and emotional responses include irritability, self-doubt, low self-esteem, disillusionment and pessimism, and (perhaps not surprisingly) obsession with one's own problems.[5]

'Burnout' is an American term which refers particularly to those who work in the caring professions and are experiencing a condition at the extreme of long-term stress, when it has become overwhelming. Not only is the term used to refer to a state of physical, emotional and mental exhaustion, but it is linked to working with emotionally demanding people, so that in 'burnout' additional symptoms appear such as blunting of emotional responsiveness, loss of interest in clients, withdrawal from colleagues and loss of meaning.[6]

Pryor reproduces a table comparing the characteristics of stress and burnout.[7] For example stress is characterized by over-engagement, burnout by disengagement; stress by over-reactive emotions, burnout by blunted emotions; stress produces disintegration, burnout demoralization; stress loss of energy, burnout loss of hope; stress hyperactivity, burnout a sense of helplessness. He also lists several stages of burnout: initial enthusiasm with unrealistically high expectations; stagnation, with the job no longer satisfying; frustration, questioning the value of the work and even one's own value; apathy, and going through the motions; and intervention—the attempt to break the cycle by restructuring relationships, seeking new skills or moving to another occupation.

Research into long-term stress, cited in Horsman,[8] indicates that the professionals who are most at risk are those who feel unsupported socially, who are unsupported by their partner, who work overhard, and who exhibit what is known as Type A behaviour: that is, those who are self-sacrificing, perfectionist, over-conscientious, who have strong sense of duty, are tightly self-controlled, obsessive, tend to suppress emotions, and have rigid standards — what psychotherapists know as the anal type of character. The profile of the particularly vulnerable is in the end so exhaustive that there is a danger that no single reader will escape self-recognition! But for the sake of completeness (and bearing in mind that it is excess of several of these features which is the true indicator), other factors identifiable in those prone to stress include people with a deep-seated sense of frustration, who are dissatisfied with work or life, who are self-deprecating, who feel helpless or alienated from society, who experience role ambiguity and are not sure what is expected of them, and those who live in an unpredictable or rapidly changing environment. A URC report adds to this already daunting list those who are over-commited in the face of intractable situations, those who cannot cope with hostility and who avoid conflict, those who are tempted to please everyone, those who have difficulty saying 'No' and who cannot protect personal boundaries for time off and the time with the family, single ministers especially women, and married women who also have to act as home-makers as well as fulfil the requirements of their paid work.[9]

Thankfully it is also possible to provide some indicators of those who are more resistant to becoming ill in the face of stressful events, although these are more concise — perhaps an indication in itself of a less crowded and complicated life. Horsman lists three 'c's': those who show *commitment,* meaning those who are able to say 'Yes' and 'No'; those who can exercise some *control,* who feel that they can act in some way to change parts of their situation; and those who accept *challenge,* who find change interesting and an incentive to growth and not a threat to security.[10] To this it is also important to add that those who are able to own their vulnerability are very different from those who hide their fear of weakness behind over-activity and the mask of omnicompetence. As the URC report puts it: 'Christian ministry is . . . concerned with enabling people to be real. It means acknowledging one's humanity, even the broken and hurting bits so that others discover it is safe for them to admit their humanity.'[11]

Both Horsman and the URC report consider in greater detail specific areas of stress and conflict. Here again there will be few ministers who do not, in some way, recognize themselves; but many of these factors are potential areas for examination in appraisal, either to be raised by the minister or to be identified by the consultant as potential areas for discussion. Appraisal provides an opportunity to try and manage some of these situations better, to help the minister to adapt, or to adapt to, the demands of the work so that they become less stressful, and pressure points can be relieved, and to increase the potential for the three 'c's' of commitment, control and challenge referred to above.

The most obvious broad area of stress is the job itself. Horsman summarizes common job stresses, drawn up from a study of secular occupations and equally valid for ministry: feelings of being out of control through excessive workload and demands, pressure of time, excess paperwork, bad working environment (is there, for instance, a proper study in which work can be done *and* also left behind?), lack of structure, lack of opportunity to learn, lack of positive feedback, poor relationships with colleagues, lack of challenge, lack of communication with superiors, role conflict and role ambiguity, lack of variety of work, boredom, lack of meaning, and (important to this book) lack of work evaluation or appraisal.

The inability to separate person from parson, which has surfaced time and again in these pages, means that stresses also arise from the particular type of work in which a minister is engaged, which has an impact upon the personality but which also may be influenced by personality. The URC report draws attention to pressure of expectations upon ministers from their congregation(s), from the wider community, and from the wider Church as well as, just as significantly, from the family and from themselves. Such expectations are exacerbated when a minister feels isolated and alone and has few friendships (difficult sometimes within a congregation without jealousies arising). Crises of faith are not uncommon in ministers, indeed may even be essential for growth in faith,[12] but these can be very painful in the face of the perceived expectations of a congregation.[13] The area of spirituality is mentioned both in Horsman and the URC report, the latter encouraging its ministers to share in retreats, quiet days and in spiritual 'direction'—even if such a term is not popular within the Reformed tradition. The need to maintain a good Christian image may therefore include the expectation, self-imposed or imposed by church and congregation, that a minister will profess and believe the true faith (as understood by a particular congregation or Church) and that he or she will be a person of prayer. If either of these areas are challenged from within when profound developmental changes occur, guilt easily arises but is not so easily assuaged. Being a model Christian may also involve suppressing some emotions, especially those which are viewed as negative (such as anger), and as such are thought to be bad to express. Where, for any of these reasons, feelings of self-esteem are undermined, one reaction is to escape the crises of identity or 'being' by getting over-involved in 'doing', and overwork can easily result.

Neither can ministry be separated from housing and other conditions of employment, and family; nor indeed should the effect of housing and levels of pay on the family be neglected. The mobility which is today part and parcel of full-time ministry involves moving jobs and moving house at regular intervals, often causing disruption to friendships and sometimes to extended family ties. Such losses are as profound (perhaps more so) for the spouse and children as they are for the minister, since unlike the minister, the family does not have a ready-made group or means of entry with which quickly to build up new relationships. Low pay (especially for those who are newly ordained) is a major source of stress, and again the spouse (which in this context almost invariably means the minister's wife) may feel conflicts between the wish to be at home for the children, and to get a job to help meet basic expenses, as well as to get away from 'living on the job', with all the pressures and expectations that may involve. The actual amount of time off, with the difficulty of affording to go away on days off and the interruptions if they stay at home, the unsocial hours and irregular routine, the telephone and doorbell ringing, and the further stresses which are imposed by expectations on both partners to demonstrate the ideal Christian marriage—all these and more illustrate the enormous potential for strain upon the minister and upon his or her family. Where the minister is a married woman and gender roles remain fixed, additional strains can occur from trying to maintain home and family; but even single women ministers suffer stress from the expectations that they will not only be the minister, but also, as a woman, the minister's wife—as the URC report says, 'preach the sermon *and* bake the cakes'.[14]

At the risk of painting a picture of gloom and doom I do not forget that many ministers cite their most important source of support and encouragement as being their spouse. Nevertheless, such a brief view of the minister and his or her family affords an opportunity for asking whether the minister provides the same degree of support for partner and children. We should not forget that long-term stress can also be experienced by the minister's spouse and family, and may indeed sometimes only be capable of being expressed through partner or family, especially where personal stress is denied by the minister. As the URC report puts it: 'All these examples indicate the factors that can, and do, disturbingly often, leave a spouse feeling trapped, helpless, hopeless and voiceless. She, or he, may have no outlet for feelings except to an already over-burdened minister partner.'[15]

Clergy partners are amongst the 'special needs' group which Horsman refers to as 'high risk':—others include single ministers, especially women in ministry; those who experience bereavement, separation or divorce; those who leave the ministry; those who retire, especially if they retire early; ministers who are homosexual; and those who work in particularly difficult ministries, such as urban priority areas. Some of these factors are, of course, not confined to ministry, but are recognized areas of stress, as indeed are many other life situations.

In one of his research instruments Pryor asked twenty professionals who counselled ministers what the main kinds of stress were in their clients. In approximate order of importance these were the tension between marriage and ministry, overwork, crises of faith, financial stress, lack of privacy in the manse, role conflict and opposed expectations, low self-esteem, and lack of care by the laity for the minister and family. The main areas listed by these counsellors in which ministers needed help were: conflict management and stress reduction, pastoral care of the minister, continuing education (academic and spiritual formation), identity and self-image, marriage and the family, financial advice, physical health and life style, and relating theological training to the parish and the world.[16]

The URC report similarly identifies ways in which stress might be better prevented and managed. The authors include the importance of practical care for self, such as physical wellbeing and relaxation; spiritual nourishment; support systems using counsellors, colleagues and superiors; in-service training and the use of the sabbatical; the local church providing active material and pastoral support; structuring the work generally and tasks specifically through the use of management skills and through firmer, more disciplined planning. For instance, they set out one model of the week, which has twenty-one sessions—morning, afternoon and evening for seven days, suggesting that a minister should work for twelve sessions, and have nine for him or herself, of which three at least should be consecutive.

It is important to acknowledge that many occupations involve risks and that ministry is not alone in this. Many careers include periods of suffering as well as of satisfaction. No-one who writes about stress and burnout in ministry is suggesting that ministry should be trouble-free or that the minister should be a consistently contented person. Pryor, for example, subtitles his study 'stress and support in the ministry of the wounded healer', and makes a point of acknowledging early in his study the importance of theological concepts such as sacrifice, self-giving in the service of others, losing one's life to find it, kenosis or self-emptying, and recognition of one's own 'foolishness' and fallibility.[17] Failure, as I noted in Chapter 5, may in the Christian gospel be a mark of faithfulness and therefore of 'success', just as failure of the therapist is recognized in psychotherapy as an essential part of the healing process.

Nevertheless, Pryor makes it clear too that effective ministry is characterized by acknowledging woundedness and the need for personal healing, by owning inabilities, and by becoming the channel for the Spirit to reach out to others. What may characterize the candidate for excessive stress, and perhaps for eventual long-term stress and 'burnout', is the inability to recognize much (or indeed any) of this gospel of the wounded healer, not only intellectually but from within the heart also. So continuous overwork, hyperactivity, and concern for marks of effectiveness may actually mask anxiety about failure, failure which is sometimes inevitable given the difficulties of the task. The wish for success for the gospel of Christ might become confused with that wish for personal success which in fact arises from a profound absence of self-worth and the need to prove oneself. The sacrifice of oneself in the apparent interests of the gospel, may for some ministers be less a way of following the example of their Lord and more a way of punishing themselves for failing to live up to their over-idealized expectations. Ultimately, although few of us are free from some of the effects of it, long-term stress is an indicator of how far we have to go to realize the gospel of acceptance and forgiveness.

The pastoral care of clergy and other ministers

Given the possibility that appraisal will, from time to time, enable a minister to express the need for further help, it is vital that those who conduct appraisals supply themselves, or preferably are supplied, with sufficient information to help them refer those who need further help to the most appropriate sources. Within the immediate locality there will probably be voluntary and statutory agencies able to offer specialist advice and expertise on a range of subjects; the

local council for voluntary service may produce a booklet
listing self-help and other groups. Where there is an adviser
for pastoral care and counselling (such posts exist in several
Anglican dioceses) such a person should be able to supply the
names of reputable counsellors and therapists. Information
on spiritual directors in the area will also be necessary, ideally
with some indication of their particular style of guidance.
Places for retreat, houses, communities and other centres for
spiritual, physical and mental refreshment are able to offer
individual help as well as organized activities. There are also
a number of organizations based in different parts of the
country offering a special ministry to clergy and religious
under stress.[18]

Thankfully there is a growing awareness of the needs of
those who previously may have been seen as the carers but
seldom understood to be in equal need of care. Thankfully
too, there is a growing understanding that attention to
personal needs, whether it takes the form of counselling,
therapy, or avenues for personal growth, often makes for a
more healthy and fruitful ministry to others. Appraisal forms
part of this process and may enable ministers to make
sufficient adjustments to life style, work patterns and
attitudes to prevent the devastating effects of those
breakdowns to which continuously unsupported and unten-
ded ministry is prone.

Notes

1. Apart from the literature referred to in the main body of this chapter,
   my attention has been drawn to the following books and reports,
   which vary in quality: W. Carr, *Brief Encounters*, SPCK, 1985, pp.
   127ff. — on the pressure of coping with expectations; *Clergy Stress and
   Burnout*, Washington DC, The Alban Institute; P. Kettle, *Staying
   Sane under Stress*, Grove Books 1987; M. Lawson, *Facing Anxiety
   and Stress*, Hodder and Stoughton 1986; *Realism and Hope*, Report of
   the Ministry Commission, Diocese of Bath and Wells 1982—4; J. A.
   Sanford, *Ministry Burnout*, Arthur James 1984; P. Tyrer, *How to
   Cope with Stress*, Sheldon Press 1980.
2. R. J. Pryor, *At Cross Purposes.* The Commission on Continuing
   Education for Ministry, Uniting Church in Australia, Victoria, 1986,
   p. 68. See also *High-Calling — High Stress* by the same author and
   publisher, 1982.

3. R. J. Pryor, *At Cross Purposes*, p. 64.
4. R. J. Pryor, ibid., p. 62.
5. Much of the information in this section, except when specifically identified, is drawn equally from: S. Horsman, *Living with Stress*, Lutterworth Press 1989; and the report *Stress in the Ministry*, The United Reformed Church 1987.
6. S. Horsman, *Living with Stress*, pp. 7—8.
7. R. J. Pryor, *At Cross Purposes*, p. 7.
8. S. Horsman, *Living with Stress*, pp. 14—15.
9. *Stress in the Ministry*, p. 7.
10. S. Horsman, *Living with Stress*, p. 16.
11. *Stress in the Ministry*, p. 8.
12. See M. Jacobs, *Towards the Fullness of Christ*, Darton Longman and Todd 1988, for a comprehensive description of the current research in faith development.
13. It is important to stress the word 'perceived' in this context, because there will be some (perhaps many) in the congregation who would welcome the minister asking the same sort of critical questions they themselves often have about their faith.
14. *Stress in the Ministry*, p. 11.
15. *Stress in the Ministry*, p. 19.
16. R. J. Pryor, *At Cross Purposes*, p. 61.
17. ibid., pp. 13—27.
18. For retreat houses, see G. Gerard, *Away from it all: a guide to retreat houses.* Lutterworth Press 1989. Other useful retreat centres include:
St Annes'—a centre for listening, Under Down, Gloucester Road, Ledbury, Herefordshire HR8 2JE. Counselling and psychotherapy.
Syon House, Angmering, West Sussex, BN16 4AG. This is run by the Vocation Sisters, and offers a service to priests and religious of any Christian denomination. It is a residential psychotherapy centre.
Heronbrook House, Bakers Lane, Solihull, West Midlands B93 8PW. Run by the Sisters of Charity of St Paul, it offers a residential therapeutic community and non-residential psychotherapy and counselling, as well as programmes in yoga, movement, psychodrama, etc. The staff group is ecumenical.
The Dympna Centre, 60 Grove End Road, London NW8 9NH. A fully ecumenical counselling centre for clergy, religious and full-time church workers.
The Society of Mary and Martha, Sheldon, Dunsford, Exeter EX6 8LE. A Christian community set up for the care of clergy and their families at times of stress and crisis. It offers day seminars on stress management, and a '12,000 mile service' week, with opportunities for relaxation and recreation.

NINE

Larger Lenses

At local level

Rather than place all the emphasis in appraisal on any one individual in isolation, I have already in earlier chapters suggested the importance of seeing the life and work of every minister in context. I have observed in Chapter 5 the danger that might arise from appraisal concentrating simply upon the minister, and in Chapter 7, following some existing appraisal schemes, I have included in the suggestions for questions that might be used in appraisal a section which asks for a brief profile of the church and local community in which a ministry might be set. If appraisal serves the interests of the individual more than the organization, then it may not be necessary to look much further than that; but if appraisal is seen as part of the ongoing review and reflection of the life of the whole church (of which the minister is only a part, even if in many cases a key part) then other forms of evaluation and audit or review (as defined in Chapter 2) need to take place. Appraisal then takes its place in the wider scheme of things, alongside what has become known as the 'parish audit' or similar local assessment, the review of churches in a region or in a diocese, and those commissions and working party reports which reflect the continuing self-examination of the churches at national level.

The diagram illustrating the concentric circles of appraisal in Chapter 1 makes it clear that my own concentration upon the individual and his or her work does not intend to exclude the outer circles which form the context in which that ministry is practised, any more than some of the more inward circles, since appraisal inevitably also includes some aspects of personal growth and development. One form of ministry where appraisal must take place in context is that of group or team ministry. In Chapter 7 I have already outlined a method of peer appraisal which could be used for teams or groups of clergy. Like Kilty,[1] the Collaborative Ministry group suggest the use of an outside facilitator or consultant, and their book *Collaborative Ministry*[2] contains useful chapters on team and group appraisal, as well as an appendix listing questions for teams and groups who might be looking for a consultant.

Most ministers still do not work in such a close way with their brother and sister clergy, although I mention below how a deanery, chapter or fraternal might engage in evaluation or review. The context in which most clergy work is the local church or parish, where the idea of review is certainly not new, even if in the past it may have been rather narrowly confined. Within the Anglican Church there has been a regular review known as 'the quinquennial'—a five-yearly survey by the archdeacon and/or rural dean, concentrating primarily upon the fabric and furnishings, finances and other material matters. Such visits have also provided some archdeacons with the opportunity of looking at the parish in a wider way. As a simple and I am sure not unique example, in one archdeaconry in the seventies the agenda for the quinquennial, as set out in the preparatory letter, certainly looked at the usual aspects such as plant and at severely practical matters like insurance; but it also featured topics such as forms of worship and resources for worship, work with particular groups of people in the church and in the secular field, matters that might be proving difficult, ecumenical relations, changes in the parish population, local affairs of concern to the church, and the relationship between the parish, the deanery and the diocese. Another Anglican diocese recommended a parish assessment every three to five years: an archdeacon or other suitable person was to spend a weekend in the parish, the purpose being 'to enable clergy and laity together in a parish or group of parishes to work out their aims and objectives and to assess how far these have been realized and then to plan again for the future.' The conclusions from this consultation were not necessarily confidential.

These two suggestions are early and less thorough examples of the 'parish audit', a term which makes its appearance in the Archbishop of Canterbury's Commission's report *Faith in the City,* where one of the appendices sets out 'an audit for the local church'.[3] The purpose of the audit is there defined as 'to help the local church to understand itself in its situation, to reflect on its purpose, and then to make plans for becoming a more effective, outward-looking and participating church'. It is suggested that a small group organizes the audit, including some sympathetic 'outsiders', and that an external consultant is invited to advise on its setting up and on the discussion of its results. The audit so described has two parts, the first being an analysis of the locality and of the church — in effect a sociological snapshot of the population and of the congregation. The second part of the audit is called 'Planning for Action', and consists of a number of questions to be asked of the local church, such as how representative its membership is, how its buildings are used, how it collaborates with other churches and other local organizations, and the kind of training that might be helpful. The answers to these questions are expected to enable objectives to emerge, from which the local congregation can decide its particular priorities for the first year following the audit.

In 1986 the annual Pastoral Council of the Roman Catholic Archdiocese of Liverpool asked its parishes to carry out such an audit. Although the booklet *Introduction to a Parish Audit*[4] draws heavily on the outline in *Faith in the City,* it is imaginatively produced and includes certain questions which are notably absent in the original on which it is based. For example, the question is asked, 'How many new members has the parish received in the last 2 years?' Another question asks about the provision for people with special needs (physical or mental handicap), including special liturgy or means of instruction. It also asks some important questions in the analysis itself which the *Faith in the City* outline leaves for the 'Planning for Action' stage. It may be necessary, for example, to find out (as the Liverpool booklet suggests) how many of the congregation are involved in local activities, and where they are so involved, before asking the rather general question (which the *Faith in the City* outline does) about whether the local church is 'seeking to be present' in various ways in the parish. In the Liverpool archdiocese the parish audit was followed up a year later with a series of questions to parishes on mission and ministry.

Another clearly produced form of audit, though not by that name, and appearing before *Faith in the City*, appears in a booklet written for the Coventry diocese, called *Steps in Pastoral Planning*. The five steps are simply but effectively stated as follows:

1. *Discovery:* this involves listing the real needs of people in the area, using other bodies for information as well as discovering specific facts, listing the needs in order of importance, and deciding how the church should respond to them, in terms of aim and action.

2. *Choosing Priorities:* here the most urgent needs are identified, as well as whether they are realistic ones for the church to tackle. Working with others is again stressed, including outside agencies, neighbouring parishes and the diocese. Others have to be kept informed of what the local church is planning. At this point a date is chosen upon which to assess and evaluate the work that is planned.

3. *Planning:* this includes stating the objectives, listing ways of achieving the aim, deciding methods, allocating tasks, fixing a date for completion, informing others, and writing a project plan.

4. *Action:* in this stage it is important to keep the objectives in mind, to meet regularly to check on progress, to let ideas and plans evolve, to be ready to adjust plans on the basis of new information, and to keep a record of progress.

5. *Assessment:* it is suggested that after each separate task within the plan the group members ask what they set out to do, where they may have gone wrong and why, what they have learned, and what the next step is. On the target date similar questions are asked in a major assessment; soon afterwards it is important to meet again, to look once more at needs that were previously put aside, or have surfaced recently, and then to begin the whole process by returning to step one.

A much more detailed form of audit can be found in the *Mission Audit Pack* produced by the Milton Keynes Christian Foundation.[5] Following an introduction on the aims and use of Mission Audit, five sections set out 36 exercises, which start with statistics and data (mapping the area, surveys, church attendance, etc), and proceed to expand awareness locally and further afield by looking at unity and community, service and witness, education and growth, and worship and spirituality. While it is suggested that the material can be used for a weekend or a six/seven week course, there is more than enough within each of the main sections to keep a church alert for several years in assessing different aspects of its mission. It is a very rich mine of questions and resources.

As far back as 1970 I conducted a similarly detailed survey, with a team of four clergy and three lay people, of the life, work and policy of a Church of England parish on a council housing estate in southern England. We were all 'outsiders' in the sense that we did not live or work in the parish. The team members each undertook a particular area for observation and analysis, such as youth work, education or the work of the clergy. One lay member (a social scientist) conducted two social surveys (using local students as interviewers), one of the general population, the other of members of the congregation. The parish clergy filled in diaries for a typical working week. This very thorough piece of research occupied all seven team members for a whole week, when they stayed in the parish, attended all the parish organizations, talked to people in and outside the church, and met daily to review the progress of their work. The survey and the subsequent report took up many hours of planning, pooling of observations, making recommendations and writing the report, which extended to over 100 pages. Without the time of all the team members being freely given, and even then without a charitable grant for expenses, such a massive venture would not have been possible for the average parish audit.

The survey yielded much valuable information about the parish. For instance, at a time when local radio was attracting attention, and the church was putting considerable energy into broadcasting, it was helpful to discover that very few people on this estate at that time listened to the radio and that they got all their local news from their daily evening newspaper, which the church did not use nearly so effectively.

The team produced a long list of recommendations, which occupied the parish council for many months.

I refer to this report, privately published mainly for the benefit of the particular parish, since it was a forerunner of the parish audit, carried through more comprehensively and with far greater expertise in the team than would be possible in most parish situations. I have no doubt that my colleagues made useful observations, and arrived at some helpful conclusions; and that the sociological analysis was more than adequate for the task. However I am not at this distance convinced that the exercise made much difference to the life of that particular local church, even though it was interesting to the clergy (and might have been of value to other clergy working in similar parishes) and it contained some interesting insights for social scientists. My doubt now lies in another direction. The report was written for a mainly working class area, what would now be called an 'urban priority area'. Yet it was as if we ourselves had made the same error that we identified in the local church with regard to local radio and local newspapers. Much effort was put into the survey, just as much effort might equally be put into a parish audit. Many facts and figures were produced. But it is likely that a simpler way, using more home-spun talent, could have yielded equally interesting and thought-provoking information; and might have more readily focused the attention of the parish council membership (who were not used to such weighty documents) upon the purpose and mission of their local church.

Both *Faith in the City* and the Liverpool booklet refer to other helpful resources for conducting an audit. It is important, however, especially in the light of the experience recounted above, to raise at this point the purpose of such a review, since it is likely to be an exercise which consumes much time and energy, especially for those who constitute the audit team. To what purpose? Given the criticisms that are made from time to time of Royal Commissions—that they delay action, that they produce long reports at great cost, but that little or nothing is done about their recommendations—it will be disappointing and demoralizing to those who conduct an audit to find that they have so much information that they do not know have the skill or the time to process it; or that they come up against yet more questions which require a further round of research; or that they make suggestions which are not taken up with any enthusiasm by those who were not part of the audit team. Although it is clear that the wide-ranging brief of the parish audit as defined in *Faith in the City* is partly designed to help objectives to emerge, the amount of material gathered from the questions may be overwhelming or too diverse to be of any real use. It is often better to limit a piece of research to a more narrowly defined area, to ask much more specific questions that might provide clearer answers that lead to 'Planning for Action', and to tackle one issue at a time.

For this reason it may be helpful to look briefly at some specific suggestions about conducting an audit or review but from a secular context. Warren Feek's *Working Effectively*[6] is a guide to evaluation techniques for use with small projects, particularly for voluntary groups or those on small funding, who might want to engage in an evaluation of their work. The aims are to help to assess how past work has gone (whether it is an active project or a discussion group), to help to make the project more effective and to plot an appropriate course for the future.

Unlike the commercial world, it is much more difficult for voluntary groups (and churches) to plot progress, since they cannot use measurements like their share of the market. There are no simple rules of thumb. Feek recommends evaluation as helping a group to look at its purpose, its goals and tasks; or to look at the nature of a problem: for instance, why is a particular group not reaching the people it wishes to? Evaluation may also help a group to look at how successful it has been or at how to use its resources in the future more effectively or more efficiently. But he observes that evaluation is made much more difficult if there is uncertainty about the principal aim of an organization or about the purpose of its work—although even realizing that there is uncertainty may in itself be a valuable finding.

It is worth noticing the difference between the *Faith in the City* audit, which concludes on the note that deep questions may be raised 'about the nature and purpose of the Church and the meaning of the Christian Gospel'[7]—that is, that a parish audit may lead to questions and, by implication, at least temporary uncertainties — and Feek's observation about uncertainty making evaluation more difficult. Might a parish have to ask the difficult questions first: 'What is our purpose? In what ways can the gospel be made known?' before it knows what information it wants from its audit, and what questions it needs to ask in order to get it?

While there are many justifiable reasons to conduct an evaluation, Feek also points out some suspect reasons. One is to use evaluation as a way of avoiding making decisions. An individual or a small group may want to delay a decision which the majority feel should be taken by saying 'We need more information on this'. A second suspect reason is to use evaluation as a way of ducking responsibility. It may be clear, for instance, that a particularly difficult decision has to be made to ask for the resignation of the leader of the youth club; but instead of carrying out the obvious action, a working party is set up to review how the youth club is working. A third suspect reason for evaluation is *simply* to produce a rosy picture to present to another group or to a funding body. Research should be entered into critically with a view to development, not as narcissistic self-congratulation.

Although evaluation can be conducted by those who work within an organization, there are disadvantages to this. Those who are already heavily involved in the local congregation may be too close to the action, may have their own axe to grind, and may have a vested interest in the outcome — particularly wanting it to show up positively. *Faith in the City* also recommends the use of outsiders. Although it may be more difficult to get such people to serve on an audit or evaluation team (and may even cost more if their expenses are to be paid) many local churches will have contact, through their congregations, with people who are not necessarily deeply involved in church work but who are willing to support it; people who have particular skills to bring to this kind of evaluation, because it is an extension of their normal work: members of planning departments, teachers of social sciences, etc. In using outsiders (especially those who have professional expertise in these matters) it is particularly important to give them a clear brief of what they are required to do, the timetable and time commitment, and to whom they are to present their finished report.

Evaluation can take many forms: questionnaires can be used; an observer may be present at a meeting; materials produced by the group or organization (such as newsletters, magazines, annual reports, minutes of meetings) can be read. Feek gives some advice on each of these aspects and has particularly valuable hints on the design of questionnaires and on sampling techniques. He puts these matters across in a simple and straightforward way, without the potential complications of statistical margins of error, which are unnecessary for a local project that is more concerned in its final report with its own interests and with self-improvement than with impressing social scientists.[8]

For those who might be put off conducting a parish audit, or even an evaluation with slender objectives, by the techniques already referred to, Feek also describes a much less formal way, but one which nonetheless provides a group (such as a house group, or a church organization) or its leader(s) with feedback and with the chance to review its activities. Simple questions are often the most effective: how do people feel the last year has gone? What has worked well? What did not work well? What lessons are there to be learned for future planning of the group and of the programme?

Feek includes an exercise called 'Talking and Acting',[9] which with adaptation might be used with any small group evaluating its activities. It begins with the creation of a list of what they have talked about or what they have done during the past so many months. The members of the group then note down and share with each other which of those activities have been of the most benefit to them and which the least benefit, and why they think or feel this. Each writes a brief paragraph on how they have changed as a result of their discussions or activities; and again they discuss or share their findings, finally arriving at an overall assessment. In the light of their discussion the group members then agree on two changes or future activities which are designed to sustain and improve the work of the group.

At area level

I do not wish to depart too far from the appraisal of ministers, and therefore need only give three different examples (out of the many that could be given from all parts of the Church) of the way in which appraisal, review or evaluation can take place beyond individual ministry and on a wider scale than the single parish. For instance, deaneries (or circuits, or a local ecumenical council of churches) may undertake a review of an area in which they all work, where pooled information and thinking may be of benefit to all. One example is of an Anglican deanery appointing a working party to look at mission, and asking each of its constituent parishes to address a number of questions about mission to the city in which they were all working, such as how the parish defines mission, what resources it lacks, how the deanery as a whole might focus on mission, etc. Given the various theologies which underpin different churches, it is important in setting up such reviews and research that there is clear definition of terms. Hence the first question, how a parish defines mission, is a crucial one, because upon that particular depend all the subsequent opinions and information.

I have in earlier chapters referred to the impact which individual appraisal may have upon the wider Church, showing up flaws or inconsistencies which need to be addressed. 'Putting one's house in order' may also be a necessary complementary step to asking individual ministers to examine their own work. One example of a diocese putting itself under review is the commissioning in 1973 of Dr John Adair, formerly of St George's House, Windsor, by the Chichester Diocesan Synod to review the administrative structures and communication of the diocese 'to enable the Church the better to fulfil its pastoral, evangelistic, social and ecumenical mission'.

If I have questioned earlier how detailed a study of attitudes and/or complex topics it is possible or desirable for a local church to make, given its limited resources, nevertheless such research might usefully be conducted at area or diocesan level. This has the advantage of being able to employ specialist expertise more efficiently, the advantage of scale—a more comprehensive picture can be gathered — and the advantage that conclusions can be more widely disseminated for the benefit of ministry as a whole. A good example of such an initiative is a questionnaire or attitude study of church members conducted in the diocese of Chester. 2840 questionnaires were returned in the whole diocese, making a very impressive sample. Church members were asked a number of questions about their own spiritual life, as well as about the way they saw the priorities of the ministry of clergy and of the Church with regard to social issues, evangelism, etc.

There were some interesting and perhaps surprising results. Some of the conclusions were not what some clergy might have expected, showing that their own priorities and the expectations of their congregations can sometimes be quite far apart. For example, the highest scoring 'main task of the church' was to maintain moral standards (and not, as we might think, pastoral care or preaching the gospel). There were some surprises too when it came to listing priorities for clergy. While it might be expected that caring for the sick, the lonely and the aged would be rated as the highest priority for clergy, and praying the second, visiting churchgoers was at the bottom of the list and training the laity the next lowest priority.

Appraisal, evaluation, reviews and research sometimes present us with new insights. I do not imply that the church members had got it wrong; but if they tend to believe one set of tasks to be the main concern of the church and the church another, or if they believe in certain priorities for their clergy and their clergy are keener on others, then at the very least it may indicate that either the clergy need to think again, or they need to set about explaining the relevance of, and reasons for, their own priorities to their people. It is possible to get a much clearer picture of trends and attitudes when they are researched at this level, using resources that are unlikely to be available in the single local church.

At national level

To complete the picture of appraisal it is necessary to include reference to the review and assessment which the Churches conduct at national level, about those matters which are of concern to the whole Church. Working parties, commissions, and study groups turn their specialist attention to weighty issues such as mission, ministry, social and ethical questions, and even to matters of doctrine. As an example of this higher level of review *Faith in the City* has already received some attention in this chapter. It is, of course, an appraisal of the nation as well as of the Church. Another example is aptly called *Industrial Mission — an Appraisal* and clearly shows the relevance of the term used throughout this book to the wider Church as well as to the individual.[10] Such large-scale topics sometimes form the subject of once-in-a-lifetime reviews, although others join the long list of reports on similar topics which have done little more than gather dust. The problem will always be that such carefully researched and discussed conclusions, while of potentially great value, have to be translated into action, often an even harder task than the original writing of them. Those who must translate such conclusions into action or decisions do not always have the same verve and fire for the issues as members of a working party, who may have invested considerable time and effort in writing their report. Those who read reports are in many cases inevitably more distant than those who write them from both the complexities of the issues and from the reasons why certain conclusions may have been reached. So while such large-scale appraisals and reviews frequently show that the churches are alive to changing needs and circumstances, ways also need to be found to translate the major issues into manageable proportions and into more immediate local dimensions. It is at ground level where ideas have to be translated into action. Congregations and clergy also have to examine the same issues (aided by the predigested material of reports) and from their own conclusions, inevitably influenced by major reports, look for their own ways to meet situations and needs. *Faith in the City*, in proposing a parish audit, clearly hoped that what the Archbishop's commission had found and experienced would become equally real for local churches and congregations.

Conclusion

The Kingdom of Heaven may be compared to a man who was going abroad and left some of his estate in the hands of his servants. To one he gave five talents—as the Authorized Version puts it—to another he gave two talents and to a third he gave one. And when he returned he asked each one what they had done with the talents which he had left them holding in trust. Two of them had invested their talents and doubled their investment. One explained that he was afraid, that he thought that the man was hard and expected miracles, such as harvests where no seed had been sown; so he had hidden his talent underground.

The parable of the talents in Matthew's Gospel,[11] as the Oxford English Dictionary makes clear, also gives us the word which designates 'mental endowment' and 'natural ability'. But whereas we may tend to see the judgement upon the man's return from abroad as a somewhat dire prefiguring of the current interest in appraisal of ministry, perhaps this story, like all good stories, can acquire a new twist of meaning for this occasion. It is not just in the faithful carrying through of the tasks and responsibilities of ministry that ordained and lay ministers, women and men, 'proclaim the death of the Lord, until he comes,' as in the eucharist.[12] Appraisal itself involves an investment which is capable of yielding rich rewards to those who are prepared to expose themselves to what at first seems like the risk of being under scrutiny and even under judgement. There are, however, those who are afraid that appraisal will do no more than expose their failure to meet savage and unrealistic demands which they have projected either onto their Lord and Master or onto their more earthly employers. Such ministers, in respect of appraisal at the very least, will no doubt wish to bury their talent underground, so that no-one, not even themselves, is given the chance to take a look at it. But those who are prepared to lay their talents on the line and look, either on their own or preferably with the aid of another's vision, in a critical and constructive way at their life and work as a servant of God, have the opportunity of finding rewards in this particular aspect of their ministry. And perhaps, in addition to the adjustments of their practice of ministry which may emerge from each appraisal, they will also have the quiet satisfaction of hearing echoes of the master's voice: 'Well done, my good and trusty servant.'[13]

Notes

1. J. Kilty, *Self and Peer Assessment and Peer Audit.* Human Potential Research Project, University of Surrey 1979.
2. The chapters are by Lawrence Reading and Don Pickard, the appendix by Denis Gardiner, in *Collaborative Ministry.* The CM Group, Loughborough, 1987.
3. *Faith in the City.* The report of the Archbishop of Canterbury's Commission on Urban Priority Areas, Church House Publishing, 1985. See Appendix A for full details of how an audit might be conducted.
4. *An Introduction to a Parish Audit.* The Pastoral Formation Office, the Roman Catholic Archdiocese of Liverpool, 1986.
5. See, for example, *Mission Audit.* The Anglican Board for Mission and Unity, Church House Publishing; *Mission Audit Pack.* Milton Keynes Christian Foundation, 4 Church Street, Wolverton, Milton Keynes MK12 5JM.
6. Warren Feek, *Working Effectively: A Guide to Evaluation Techniques.* Bedford Square Press 1988.
7. *Faith in the City,* p. 372.
8. W. Feek, *Working Effectively,* pp. 20−3.
9. ibid., p. 31.
10. *Industrial Mission − an Appraisal.* Church of England Board for Social Responsibility 1987.
11. Matt. 25.14−30.
12. 1 Cor. 11.26 (NEB).
13. Matt. 25.21 (NEB).

Bibliography

Barger, G. et al., *The Institutional Chaplain — structures for accountability and assessment*. University of Nebraska at Omaha (unpublished research).

Brinkerhoff, D. W. and Kanter, R. M., *Formal Systems of Appraisal of Individual Performance: some considerations, critical issues and application to non-profit organizations*. Institution for Social and Policy Studies, Yale University, 1979.

Carr, W., *Brief Encounters*. SPCK 1985.

Clergy Stress and Burnout. The Alban Institute, Washington DC.

Elton, L., *Teaching in Higher Education: appraisal and training*. Kogan Page 1987.

Etzioni, E., *A Comparative Analysis of Complex Organizations*. New York, The Free Press of Glencoe, 1961.

Faith in the City. The report of the Archbishop of Canterbury's Commission on Urban Priority Areas, Church House Publishing, 1985.

Feek, W., *The Way We Work*. Leicester, National Youth Bureau, 1982.

Feek, W., *Working Effectively: A Guide to Evaluation Techniques*. Bedford Square Press 1988.

Forshaw, E., *Mis-managing the Church?* Southwell and Oxford Papers on Contemporary Society 1988.

Foskett, J. and Lyall, D., *Helping the Helpers*. SPCK 1988.

Guidelines to a Staff Development Policy. Leicester, In Service Training and Education Panel (INSTEP) and The Council for Education and Training in Youth and Community Work (CETYCW) 1985.

Hartung, B., 'The Capacity to Enter Latency in Learning Pastoral Psychotherapy'. *Journal of Supervision and Training in Ministry*, vol. 2, Chicago, Illinois, 1979.

179

Hiscox, R., Gammell, J. and Raybould, C., *Report of the Working Group on Appraisal and Assessment.* Church of England Continuing Ministerial Education Committee, May 1988.

Horsman, S., *Living with Stress.* Cambridge, Lutterworth Press, 1989.

Industrial Mission — an Appraisal. Church of England Board for Social Responsibility, 1987.

Jacobs, M., *The Presenting Past.* Open University Press 1986.

Jacobs, M., *Still Small Voice.* SPCK 1982.

Jacobs, M., *Swift to Hear.* SPCK 1985.

Jacobs, M., *Towards the Fullness of Christ.* Darton, Longman and Todd 1988.

Kadushin, A., 'Games People Play in Supervision'. *Social Work [USA]* 13:3, 23–32, 1968.

Kettle, P., *Staying Sane under Stress.* Bramcote, Nottingham, Grove Books, 1987.

Kilty, J., *Self and Peer Assessment.* Human Potential Research Project, University of Surrey, 1978.

Kilty, J., *Self and Peer Assessment and Peer Audit.* Human Potential Research Project, University of Surrey, 1979.

Lawson, M., *Facing Anxiety and Stress.* Hodder and Stoughton 1986.

Marks and Spencer Training Department, *Appraisals.* Marks and Spencer plc. 1987.

Mead, L., *Evaluation: of, by, for and to the clergy.* The Alban Institute, Washington DC.

Mills, J. and Nelson, J. (eds), *Explorations into Parish Ministry: a Guide to Joint Work Consultation.* Liverpool Diocese 1983.

Mission Audit. The Anglican Board for Mission and Unity, Church House Publishing.

Ministry to Priests: a study of effectiveness. Washington DC, The Center for Human Development, 1983.

Oswald, R., 'Clergy Evaluation: a map of the minefield'. *Action Information*, Washington DC, The Alban Institute 1988.

Pryor, R. J., *At Cross Purposes.* The Commission on Continuing Education for Ministry, Uniting Church in Australia, Victoria, 1986.

Pryor, R. J., *High-Calling — High Stress*. The Commission on Continuing Education for Ministry, Uniting Church in Australia, Victoria, 1982.

Randell, G., Packard, P. and Slater, J., *Staff Appraisal*. Institute of Personnel Management, 3rd edn 1984.

Realism and Hope. Report of the Ministry Commission, Diocese of Bath and Wells, 1982—4.

Report on Sector Ministries. The National Society (Church of England) for the Promotion of Religious Education 1983.

Rudge, P., *Ministry and Management*. Tavistock Publications 1968.

Sanazaro, P. J. et al., 'Medical Audit'. *British Medical Journal* 1, 272, 1974.

Sanazaro, P. J. et al., 'Competence to Practice'. *British Medical Journal* 2, 1218, 1976.

Sanford, J. A., *Ministry Burnout*. Arthur James 1984.

Searles, H., 'Problems of Psycho-analytic Supervision'. *Collected Papers on Schizophrenia and Related Subjects*, Hogarth Press 1965.

Stress in the Ministry. The United Reformed Church 1987.

Taylor, M., 'Theology and Collaborative Ministry', *Collaborative Ministry,* Loughborough, CM Group, 1987.

Those having torches . . . teacher appraisal: a study. HMSO/ Suffolk Education Department 1985.

Trasler, J., *Performance Appraisal*. The Council for Education and Training in Youth and Community Work.

Tyrer, P., *How to Cope with Stress*. Sheldon Press 1980.

Walrond-Skinner, S., *Family Matters*. SPCK 1988.

Waton, A., 'The Politics of Appraisal'. *AUT Bulletin*, September 1987.

Index

ACCM (Advisory Council for the Church's Ministry) 71, 101-2, 132
accountability 3, 111, 133
action plan 135, 167-8, 171
Adair, J. 174
Advisers in Pastoral Care and Counselling 54, 79, 163
affirmation 5-6
aims and objectives *see* objectives
Alban Institute 99, 113
anal character 157
appointments 58, 82, 95, 101
appraisal: content of 36-8, 68-71, 100-1, 136-45; definition of 19; existing schemes within the Church 51-76; forms for 36-7, 39-41, 69, 136-41; frequency of 42-3, 45, 56, 73, 75, 107, 134; in industry etc. 18-49; models used by the Church 62-3; problems about 43-9, 93-112, 119-24; procedures for 38-42, 72-4, 128-30, 133-6, 145; purpose of 23-31, 57-62; terms for 19-23, 57; *see also* assessment; review; self-appraisal

appraisers 6-8, 18, 31-6, 41, 43-4, 63-8, 74, 99, 100, 107, 111-12, 116, 118-31, 133-6, 141, 149, 158, 162; characteristics of 124-8; *see also* consultants
armed services chaplains 55
assessment 51-3, 168; definition of 19; *see also* appraisal
Association of University Teachers 24-5, 28, 30, 35, 41, 47, 40; *see also* universities
Aston scheme 52, 71
audit 19-20, 22, 69; definition of 20; *see also* parish audit

bishops 5-6, 15, 54-6, 60, 64-6, 74-6, 83, 94, 103, 107-8
Body of Christ 3-5, 17, 31, 60, 102-6
Brinkerhoff, D. W. and Kanter, R. M. 24, 26, 38, 44, 46-7, 49-50
Brown, Thomas E. 88
burnout 150, 155-62

career development 62, 101, 107-8; *see also* developmental needs

Church of England 51-76
Centre for Human
    Development 78-87, 91-2
Centre for Professional
    Development in Ministry 88
Civil Service 18, 31, 33, 41,
    62-3, 93
coercive structures 104
collaborative ministry 3-4, 95,
    166, 178
Committee of Vice-Chancellors
    and Principals 25, 28, 50
compulsory appraisal 42, 57,
    65, 73, 98-9, 133
confidentiality 7, 73, 149-50,
    166
confrontation 32, 44, 96,
    126-7, 152
congregation, involvement of
    6, 94-7, 166-7
consultants 22, 34-5, 64, 67,
    72, 99, 145, 166, 172;
    definition of 21; *see also*
    appraisers
consumers, appraisal by 67-8,
    96
Continuing Ministerial
    Education Officers 54, 74,
    79
counselling 11, 13, 49, 57, 75,
    91, 100, 112, 115, 117,
    124-5, 127, 151-2, 163-4;
    see also psychotherapy
Creation story 2, 6

Davey, J. 55-6
deans, rural and area 65, 72,
    107
deployment of clergy 58
developmental needs 26, 27,
    30, 46, 59-61, 71, 77, 82,

86, 89-90, 101, 127, 129,
    140, 165
difficulties: in appraisal 43-9,
    93-112, 119-24; personal
    12, 59; in institutions 49
diocesan: profile 81-2, 84;
    review 87
*Directory of Training
    Opportunities* 132
dismissal 62, 128
Dostoevsky, F. 122

education, appraisal in 18-19,
    34, 44, 49; *see also*
    universities
Edward King Institute 78-9,
    84, 87-92
eschatology 3-5, 112
Etzioni, E. 104, 113
eucharist 177
evaluation 23, 83, 90, 168,
    171-3, 175; definition of
    20; of appraisal 45, 74,
    129-31, 146-7; *see also*
    review
evaluation forms 34, 52, 130-1
expectations 7, 16, 59, 66,
    139, 158-9, 164, 175

facilitator *see* appraisers;
    consultants
failure 3, 101-2, 162
faith development 101, 113,
    159, 164
Faith in the City 49, 20,
    166-7, 170-2, 176, 178
family, minister's 7, 12-13, 54,
    71, 100-1, 139, 140, 157,
    159-61
feedback from appraisal 82,
    149-50, 173

Feek, W. 113, 171-3, 178
financial considerations 13, 111-12, 134, 144, 172
follow-up 136
Forshaw, E. 77, 103, 107-8, 113
Foskett, J. 20, 49, 119-20, 132
French Revolution 48
Freud, S. 117
frustrations in ministry 59, 138-9, 142, 151-7

goals *see also* objectives
grace 2-3
grievance interviews 127
group appraisal 33-4, 66, 133, 173; *see also* peer appraisal
guilt 9, 114, 118

halo effect 44
Hardaker, I. 49, 57, 75, 77
Hartung, B. 117-18, 132
Herbert, T. 113
hierarchical appraisal 64-6, 70, 103-4
Hiscox, R. et al. 56-7, 63-6, 75, 77, 128, 132
Horsman, S. 157-60, 164
hospital chaplains 67-8
housing 13, 140, 159, 161

ideals 115, 121
Ignatius of Loyola 155-6
industrial mission 67, 176, 178
inner self 10-11; *see also* personal life
in-service training *see* training
Institute of Personnel Management 26, 50

interview, types of 127-8
interviewing 41, 112, 114-31, 125-30
Introduction to a Parish Audit 167-8, 170, 178
isolation of clergy 86

Jacobs, M. 113, 132, 164
Jarratt Report 32, 50
job description 38, 108-11, 135, 137
Joint Work Consultation ix, 54-5, 57, 61, 63, 65, 68-70, 72, 74-7, 113, 148
judgement 1, 2-5, 114-17, 121, 125

Kadushin, A. 119-24, 126, 132
Kilroy, B. 113
Kilty, J. 31, 33-4, 50, 144-8, 166, 178

laity 7, 95, 153; *see also* congregation; lay ministers
latency mode 117
lay ministers x, 15-16, 95, 137, 139, 142-4, 154-5; 177; *see also* readers, appraisal of
learning 117-19
Lewis, C. 77
listening skills 126
long-term objectives 14, 141
Lyall, D. 20, 49, 119-20, 132

management in the Church 63, 77, 93-4, 102-8, 151, 161
Marks and Spencer 28, 41, 50, 107, 113
Mead, L. 113

medicine 18, 49, 68
ministerial review 57; *see also*
  appraisal
Ministry to Priests Programme
  55, 78-87, 90-2, 150
mission 58, 103, 134, 174
mission audit 168-9, 178
moral reasoning 85
motivation 28, 141

Nelson, J. 125, 132
non-profit organizations 46-7,
  63
non-stipendiary ministry
  (NSM) 151-3
normative structures 104

objectives 38, 58, 70, 89, 97,
  125, 129, 135, 140-1, 167,
  171; *see also* long-term
  objectives; short-term
  objectives
oedipal problems 118
Oswald, R. 48, 50, 95-6, 98,
  102, 113

parish audit 16, 20, 97, 135,
  165-73, 178
pastoral care of clergy 59-60,
  66, 77, 161-3
pastoral counselling *see*
  counselling
peer appraisal 32-3, 35, 66,
  72, 133, 144-8; *see also*
  group appraisal
peer support 80-1, 89, 147
personal life 10-12, 44, 68,
  70-1, 79-80, 86, 89, 93,
  99-101, 121, 140, 147, 158,
  161

personal development *see*
  developmental needs
pilot schemes 42, 48, 72, 74
prayer 84
preferment 29; *see also*
  appointments; promotion
priorities 168
prison chaplains 55
Probation Service 27, 30, 36,
  42, 45
promotion 25, 45, 59, 61-2,
  108
Pryor, R. 151, 156, 161-4
psychological tests 78, 80, 82,
  84-5, 88
psychotherapy 11-12; *see also*
  counselling
punishment reviews 27

quinquennial inspection 9,
  166
questionnaires 88, 136-41,
  145, 173, 175

radio, local 169
Randell, G. et al. 27-30, 35,
  37, 50, 126-8, 129-32
rating scales *see* scales
Raybould, C. 148
readers, appraisal of ix, 15,
  142-4, 154-5
recency effect 39, 44
Reiss, R. 113, 132, 148
resistance to appraisal 98,
  119-24
resource management 28-9
resources 128, 132, 154,
  162-4, 175
responsibilities of job 110,
  137, 143
retreat 80, 82, 87, 163-4

review 5, 8, 10, 109, 146-7,
    165, 171-3, 175-6;
    definition of 19-20;
    organizational 23, 29-30,
    47, 58-9, 87; performance
    23, 25-8, 30, 46, 54, 60-1;
    potential 23, 28-9, 37, 61,
    82; reward 23-7, 61-2;
rewards of ministry 151-5,
    178
Ripon College, Cuddesdon 52
roles of clergy 89, 158, 161
Roman Catholic Church 55,
    78-87, 167-8, 170
Rudge, P. 104-6, 113

St Albans ministry training
    course 53
St John's College, Nottingham
    53
sampling techniques 173
satisfaction in ministry 138,
    151-5
scales 36, 38, 43, 70, 101
Searles, H. 119, 132
sector ministries 55, 58,
    69-70, 71-2, 77, 113,
    150-1
self-appraisal, self-assessment
    12, 31-2, 35-6, 52, 64, 84,
    88, 114, 116, 136
self-criticism 12, 32, 114-118,
    159
self-deception 4
self-perception 85, 129, 135
sex 156
short-term objectives 59,
    140-1
sin 4, 9
Social Responsibility Officer
    110

soul friend 80
spiritual direction 8-9, 11, 13,
    57, 91, 100, 140, 151, 159,
    163
spirituality 91, 99, 140, 150,
    161, 163-4, 169
Steps in Pastoral Planning
    168
stewardship 2-3, 5-6
stress 49, 150, 155-62, 164;
    those at high risk 160
success 2-3, 101-2, 118, 162
succession planning 28-9, 62
superego 114-17
supervision 20-3, 33, 36-7, 43,
    50, 106, 119, 124;
    definition of 21
support 22, 41, 61, 90, 111,
    127; definition of 21; groups
    81, 83
systems theory 5

Talents, Parable of the 177-8
Taylor, M. 3-4, 17
theological colleges/courses
    12-13, 51-3, 71
theology and appraisal 2-6
training: 101, 128, 151, 161;
    needs 7, 30, 37, 54, 58, 61,
    74, 108, 140-1; of
    appraisers 44, 72, 74,
    111-12, 130-1; post-
    ordination 53-4, 67
Transactional Analysis 115
Trasler, J. 26, 38, 42, 50, 126,
    132
Type A behaviour 157
typologies of ministry 104-6;
    charismatic 105; classical
    105; human relations model

105; systemic 105-6;
  traditional 104-5

unconscious self 10
United Reformed Church 55,
  157-62, 164
universities 24-5, 30, 32, 35,
  40, 42-3, 45-7, 62
urban priority area 160, 170
utilitarian structures 104

vocation 108-9

voluntary organizations 18-19,
  26-7, 171; *see also* non-
  profit organizations
voluntary appraisal 72-3, 98-9,
  133-4; *see also* compulsory
  appraisal

youth and community services
  19, 26-7, 30, 43, 48, 50, 64,
  66-7, 77